"Number is the most momentous idea in the history of human nature."

-John Zerzan-

FREDERICK J. VELDMAN, PH.D.

THEURGY AND NUMBERS
~Purification, Liberation and Salvation of the Soul~

Waning Moon Publications

COLD SPRING, U.S.A.
2010

First edition published by:

Waning Moon Publications LLC

Post Office Box 79

Cold Spring, NY 10516

USA

waningmoonpublications.com

Library of Congress Control Number: 2010920259

ISBN-13: 978-0-9823549-4-0

ISBN-10: 0-9823549-4-0

Author contact information: fjveldman@yahoo.co.uk

Cover page and illustrations: FS Gillespie (gillespiefs@yahoo.com)

TABLE OF CONTENTS

ACKNOWLEDGEMENTS

The author wishes to acknowledge the following individuals:

- Ruth Nielsen, mentor and "mother," that introduced me to the Pythagorean Number System, as a Gift;
- Doug Pridgen, that served as a catalyst towards acquiring a deeper understanding of the different philosophical concepts discussed in this treatise;
- Don Webb, for listening, wise words, and valuable feedback;
- Patty Hardy, for guidance and additional support;
- Members of the Order of the Trapezoid, for their strengthening of the Black Flame;
- Members of the Order of Xnum, for debate and valuable input;
- My friend Joe Botha, for technical revision of the document;
- My partner, Frank, for his lasting moral support, patience and assistance with the graphics and art;
- Andy and Erika Gillespie, for their warmth, support and patience;
- Tanwyn Eacott, for her ongoing friendship, mentoring and support.

FOREWORD

"Divine Work in a Postmodern World"

We live in an age of competing world-views and philosophical perspectives. The scientist is inclined to view it as an age of progress, while the Hindu sees it as a Kali-Yuga, Thelemites the Aon of Horus and New Age enthusiasts the Age of Aquarius. It is an age in which the man* of reason might view his spiritually inclined neighbour as superstitious and irrational, while the man of spirit may consider his intellectually inclined brother to be shallow and misguided. There is a third class of person - those who see both views as partial and limited in scope. All three have struggled with each other since the dawn of our species - sometimes intellectually and productively, other times physically and destructively. All three can benefit from the contents of this book, improving themselves and the world by hard work.

The man of reason may find the emphasis on arithmetic and philosophical theory appealing, while the man of spirit might find the emphasis on theology and magical practice to their liking. A third class of person will see the necessity of both - how and why they fit together to form an integrated system of intellectual enlightenment and spiritual attainment. These are of course general classifications, as most people don't fit exclusively into one class or another. Working through the system involves a process of discovering which qualities are lacking, correcting the deficiencies and living the life proper to a rational being. The examined life mandated by Socrates and the life of flourishing (Gk. *eudaimonia*) envisioned by Aristotle are primary examples of the ideal.

Just as medical doctors diagnose physical health, prescribing what is needed to achieve and maintain it, theurgists diagnose

---

* *Masculine pronouns are used for convenience and are in no way intended to exclude women.*

v

spiritual health, prescribing what is needed to achieve and maintain it. If you value your spiritual health and you want the responsibility of achieving and maintaining it for yourself, you might consider the practice of Theurgy as a viable path to that end. This book provides the seeker with an encouraging first step, a life-long guide and handy reference volume in that direction. As the author is a Left-Hand Path Adept and Initiate within a true Hermetic Order, the theory and practice of Theurgy is presented from that perspective. These terms will be defined for the sake of clarity.

The Left-Hand Path is a path of spiritual development involving election and isolation. Election means it is a deliberately chosen path of iconoclasm, the breaking of cultural taboos, for the purpose of liberating oneself from habitual patterns of thought and behaviour. This iconoclasm does not involve illegal activities and such activities are neither encouraged nor endorsed by true Initiates of the Left-Hand Path. The path is one of isolation in that liberation enables the Initiate to identify themselves with and assimilate themselves to their own indwelling divinity. Within a Left-Hand Path context, isolation refers to the singling out of essential qualities, not to alienation in the sense of becoming a sociopath. An ethic of rational self interest is practiced as a safeguard against exclusive identification with the sensual and perceptual levels of being.*

Initiation within a true Hermetic Order consists of four phases, as taught by the Μαγος Μυστηριον[1] to his students:
- First is an abiding enthusiasm rooted in personal affinity for the mysterious object of one's desire. This mystery is the guiding principle that initiates and nurtures the quest and is the source of knowledge and power.

---

* *Referred to as the id-monster phenomenon after the film 'Forbidden Planet.'*

---

[1] Flowers, Stephen E. *Hermetic Magic.* York Beach, ME: Samuel Weiser, 1995. xix.

- The next phase is to do the actual work required to win this knowledge, a study of primary texts from the first five centuries CE. Chief among these are *The Corpus Hermeticum* and *The Greek Magical Papyri*, along with scores of supplementary texts. The Hellenic (Indo-European) and Egyptian (Semito-Hamitic) cultures being the two primary (informing) streams of the Tradition, a basic education in Classical studies and Egyptology lends itself to a deeper, richer, more profound experience and insight. Here the reader may be wondering what benefit there is in studying ancient texts. Due to the mysterious nature of the work, a direct answer cannot be given. Such can only be won by individual effort. However, an indirect answer or clue can be given by suggesting that their value resides not in how old they are, but in virtue of the fact that they are original, immediate products of the Tradition and therefore closer to the eternal source.
- Following the phase of objective scholarship is the creation of a personal synthesis based on reflective, deep thought. Here the formal information is internalized and vivified with content and meaning, as the spirit of the law is breathed into the letter of the law. The aim of this synoptic phase is to bring integrity and coherence to the work while filtering out the non- essentials.
- Next comes the phase of testing by doing, by actually putting what has been wrought into practice. This brings further refinement to theory and as a consequence improves practical application. Persistence in this will inevitably lead to the development of a hermeneutic and exegesis, a personal teaching that the individual is tasked to pass on to others, which then leads to further testing and refinement. This then serves as the means by which the Tradition intuited during the phase of objective scholarship is passed on from one generation of Initiates to the next.

This book is the product of one who has undergone this process and who of necessity seeks to pass on their knowledge to those wishing to embark upon their own Initiatory journeys. This keeps the Tradition alive and flourishing so that others may explore the wonders of their own divinity. This is the Hermetic imperative and the focus of this work - the theory and practice of Theurgy.

What is Theurgy? The word is Greek and translates into English as "divine work." This tool can be used for good or ill, to aspire to the highest and best or to surrender one's intellectual autonomy - to Come into Being[2] or to merge with the all. PAKERBETH, which means to rise up to and embody a divine state, is a formula in *The Greek Magical Papyri* and is derived from the Egyptian *paχer-neter*, which translates to "working-as-the-god."[#] The essential identity of these concepts with that of Theurgy are obvious to the insightful. The perspectives and aims presented in this book are those of the Left-Hand Path and it is within this context that the "divine work" of Theurgy is intended to operate.

Douglas Pridgen
Order of Xnum, Grand Master
One of the Seventy Two

---

* Xeper, the Word of the Aon of Set, which encompasses both being and becoming.

---

[2] Webb, D. *The Seven Faces of Darkness, Practical Typhonian Magic.* Austin, Texas: Runa-Raven, 1996. p.7

AUTHOR'S PREFACE

Almost two thousand six hundred years ago, one of the greatest minds of all times, Pythagoras, was teaching Greek philosophers a system that even today, influences religious thought. It is not certain where Pythagoras received his training. Some sources suggest that it was from the Egyptian priest-philosophers, others suggest it was of his own. Yet, what is important for us is not the source of his teaching, but rather that in this discrepancy we find proof of how flexible the system is. Greek and ancient Egyptian civilizations were worlds apart.

Pythagorean thought is not a religion. It provides a framework within which religion can be applied. Yet, Pythagorean thought of antiquity, contained a lifestyle and was not confined only to religion, but also manifest within politics, trade, medicine, the arts, music, etc. My own experience is that the high degree of success we achieve by applying Pythagorean principles in any one of these faculties warrants a transfer of these principles also to the other faculties of our existence. Soon it does become a lifestyle.

Herein is discussed the application of Neoplatonic philosophy, including all of its possibilities, within a Pythagorean framework. Neoplatonism then, becomes fundamentally a religion. In general, religious systems are more question than answer. They seem surrounded by a virtual penumbra of wonder. To be human at all is to live in an ill-lit zone of imponderables: Why am I alive at all? Where did I come from and where am I going? How am I to conduct my life in a world as confused as this? Why is there something rather than nothing? In addition, what is more puzzling and disturbing than the problem of death, and its companion, evil? In essence, Pythagorean thought is a system of understanding, rather than that of question or answer.

Every enquiry proceeds by means of a comparative relation, whether an easy or a difficult one. The United States of

America, the Solar System, the Mind of God, everything has an address somewhere within the universe, except for the universe itself. Yet, what could be closer for us, than our own consciousness? Plotinus spoke of the real as One; the only way we could observe it is to be separate from it, and to be separate from the One is to pluralize it, in which case it is not the One we are observing. This is why numbers become an important aspect of our investigation.

Pythagoras provides us with a system with which we can make discoveries that are based on logic, more so than any other existing system. It is free from dogma and/or human intervention. To know God, is to be God; therefore, not being God, all things divine will remain forever hidden from us. Theurgy, as a system of magic, gives us an opportunity to become this god. The ultimate nature of the world finally becomes accessible to the rational mind. Yet, it is only as a god that we can explore and learn about these mysteries.

The longer the quest for answers continues, the greater the mysteries that inspire it. That is, the object of the quest becomes increasingly less intelligible even as the quest becomes more urgent. There is something at stake, something that matters to those engaged in it, that is critically important to them, something that they already find perplexing and in need of understanding, even if the understanding is only preliminary.

At one point Simplicio sighs, "When shall I cease from wondering?" No matter how many *truths* we may accumulate, our knowledge falls infinitely short of *the* truth.

Walk the Path and Become!
(Solvitur ambulando!)

Frederick J. Veldman

South Africa, January 2010

x

OPERATIONAL DEFINITIONS

Anthropic Principle

To explain the existence of the universe, we must also explain our own existence. The anthropic principle is the collective name for several ways of asserting that physical and chemical theories, especially astrophysics and cosmology, need to take into account that there is life on Earth, and that one form of that life, *Homo sapiens*, has attained rationality.

Cosmogony

The study of the origin, and sometimes the development, of the universe or the solar system, in astrophysics, religion, and other fields. It includes any specific theory, model, myth, or other account of the origin of the universe or creation of the universe.

Cosmology

A cosmology is the conceptual framework of the individual, school of thought, or whole culture by means of which the world is understood.[3] It is the study of the Universe in its totality, and by extension, humanity's place in it.

Black Magic

There are many different categories of Black Magic. For standardization purposes, we refer in this manuscript to Black Magic as a change brought about in the Subjective Universe of the individual, which, in turn, could have an effect on the Objective Universe of the individual. This change is directed by the individual Will. It is what some call Higher or Greater Black Magic (not Sorcery). This excludes "trickery," which is the application of obscure physical or behavioral laws within the realm of the Objective Universe.

---

[3] Flowers, S.E. 1995. (p. 47)

Good and Evil

*"For all the Gods are good, and invariably the causes of good;
and all of them are uniformly convolved to one good,
according to the beautiful and good alone."*

-Iamblichus-

Pythagoreanism teaches us to think outside the realm of dualism. It forces us to revisit our definition of good and evil. In general, when we talk of evil, we link our description to that of adversity, as represented by Satan, Set, Lucifer, etc. Yet, it is very important to acknowledge that evil, as defined by Pythagoreans and Theurgists, means nothing but "unknowing." Evil are those that do not aspire to become as a God! No God, within the realm of this definition, can be evil! The only identifiable entities that exert evil qualities are a specific sub-group of daemons.

Evil daemons assume the appearance of Gods and good daemons. They are an abundant evil-producing tribe. In effect, they misguide the magician and cause him or her to wonder away from the Gods. Working with evil daemons requires that the worshipper should be just, because he assumes the appearance of one belonging to the divine genus, but he is subservient to what is unjust, because he is depraved. When we detect any falsehood in predictions, we refer this to the intervention by evil daemons.

Left-Hand Path (LHP)

The LHP is one of consummation where the magician approaches one or more archetypes (gods), using it as an image to become in the like of. The LHP magician is free to believe that these archetypes are mere manifestations of the sub-conscious, or that they actually exist. It does not change the way in which we approach them. Within this model, the archetype can be present, but does not take control over the life of the individual. That is, the LHP means the individual takes sole responsibility for their actions and their quest. It is therefore, not a system of submission, such as in the case of the Right-Hand Path.

Noetic

The word "noetic" comes from Greek νοητικός, for "intellective or of the intellect" (ultimately derived from the Greek word voῦς, noûs, is "intellect, higher mind, thought"). It is associated with the direct knowing or intuition of noesis.

Objective and Subjective Universe

The Self finds itself in a Universe that comprises of the Subjective and Objective realms. The Objective Universe contains space and time and is independent of the Self. When the Self ceases to exist, the Objective Universe maintains it structure. The Subjective Universe is a dependent of the Self and a product of the individual perception of the Objective Universe.

Paradigm

A school of cultural thought or pattern of thought by which individuals and even whole cultures live. Each of us is guided by an internal paradigm. It defines the way we perceive Man and the Universe. From the fourth century through the early of the Nineteenth Century, a biblically based Christian worldview was the social norm. This period was followed by that during which Science was used as the norm to explain all phenomena.

Pseudepigraphia

Pseudepigrapha (from the Greek: ψευδής, pseudēs, "false" and ἐπιγραφή, epigraphē, "inscription") are texts whose claimed authorship is unfounded.

Soteriology

Soteriology is the branch of theology that deals with salvation. It is derived from the Greek sōtēṛion "salvation" (from sōtēr "savior, preserver") + logos (word)]. The term itself can be used to refer to any kind of religion, and no savior figure or figures are required. Soteriology is a key factor that distinguishes religion from philosophy.

The Self

The Self is a collective term, which refers to all aspects and levels of the individual existence.

Theurgy

Theurgy means 'divine-working'.[4] It works in harmony with the gods, as well as with the laws of the objective universe, or at least with the characteristics of the powerful subjective universes that surround the Theurgist, and that are called gods, angels, daemons, and so on. Theurgy is a series of rituals and operations aimed at recovering the transcendent essence from which man emanates, by retracing the divine 'signatures' through the layers of being.

---

[4] Flowers, S.E. 1995. (p.103)

PART I

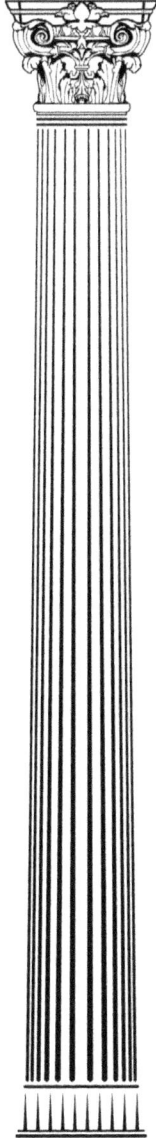

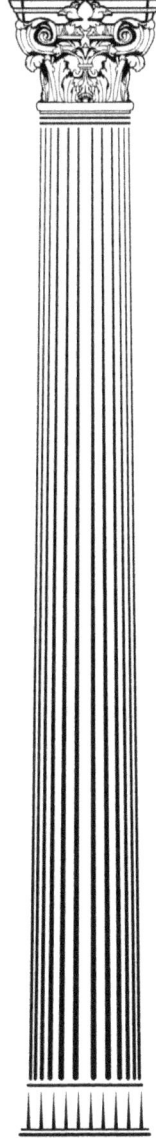

A HISTORY
of
PYTHAGOREAN
NUMBER MYSTICISM

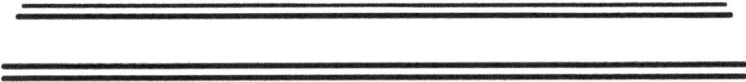

"Beginning is half of All"

-Pythagoras-

INTRODUCTION

"Number is the purest and most perfect expression of esoteric knowledge, and we must return to those bare bones"

-R.A. Schwaller de Lubicz-

The exact origin of Pythagorean philosophy is uncertain, but as depicted in its name, Pythagoras received credit for most of it. As one gains a better understanding of Pythagorean thought, it becomes evident why its origin is so difficult to trace. The system itself, through its efficiency and effectiveness, gained so much support, that almost every civilized society applied, at least in part, its basic principles to guide both the individual and the group. Proof of this lies scattered not only in the ancient writings of the Greeks, or even Italians, but also in the monumental remains of ancient Egypt.

Pythagorean principles represent a dedicated lifestyle, based on strict codes that were all-encompassing, and addressed every aspect that defines us as both material and spiritual beings. Yet, Pythagorean principles never prescribed these codes themselves, but rather the guidelines towards which the individual approached them. Pythagoreanism is therefore, free from dogma or cultural restrictions and it is for this reason that the evidence, on which we base our analysis of this lifestyle, lies scattered all across the world- in the Egyptian remains and later expounded on in the Greek literature. Yet, long after Pythagoras has died and the Egyptian civilization came to an end, the Neoplatonic philosophers of Greece synthesized Pythagorean principles with that of their own, bringing to the Western world what we have today. Here, we have interwoven with Pythagorean and Neoplatonic philosophy, a system that fits perfectly into our contemporary Left-Hand Path understanding of the universe.

We are not concerned here with the Pythagorean way of life, but rather the Pythagorean Number System, which is but one of its facets. The Pythagorean Number System, on which all our later magical inventions rely, provides the basic framework on which we can also base all future investigations into the unknown. In order to grasp these principles, it is important to provide some basic background regarding those from whom we draw its practice. We first indentify the major role-players and then, look closer at their own understanding of the universe. In this, some useful keys will become apparent as the reader becomes more acquainted with the Number System.

ORIGIN

"Knowledge left the temple first through the ideas of Greek visitors such as Tahles, Pythagoras, and Plato,: however modified by the sharpness of Greek concepts, it came back to establish its presence at the roots of Western philosophy; a second path was through Egyptian Gnosticism and heretical Christianity; a third through the images of the Tarot whose cards, just as surely as the Emerald Tablet of Hermes Trismegistus, are said to portray the structure of the sacred science of the Egyptians."

-Andre Vandenbroeck, Al-Kemi-

The Neoplatonic Philosophers originally used Pythagorean Number Mysticism as an approach to solve the mysteries of the origin of the universe. The exact origin of the Number System is unknown, but speculated to be as old as the Egyptian civilization, even though written proof of it is only found much later in the Greek literature. Although there is little doubt that classical Greek society contributed immensely to the advancement of civilization, particularly in art, architecture and philosophy, the idea that the Greeks were never influenced by other cultures (notably Egypt), is largely unsustainable, since it is clear from ancient texts that those cultures did not live in isolation.[5] Yet, for us, in the present, the exact origin of the System is irrelevant, since both the Greek and Egyptian synthesis contributes towards our current understanding of the System. The Greek literature provides a thorough theoretical basis for understanding of the System, whereas Egyptian archeology shows how Pythagorean principles were applied in practice, by an entire society. In this respect, it is very important to realize that one cannot discriminate against one or the other, but that they form a complement necessary to see as a whole.

The Egyptian Origin

Some authors reason that the Pythagorean Number Mysticism, is Egyptian in origin.[6] Much of this mysticism corresponds to the underlying philosophy that explains, in part, the essence of Egyptian art, science and religion and is suspected to be more than just mere coincidence. Moreover, as work goes on in the various fields of modern science, in anthropology, archaeology, linguistics, metaphysics and many other disciplines, new facts keep coming to light and new theories keep being advanced that directly and indirectly relate to this Symbolic understanding of ancient Egypt. Had the Egyptians possessed both their high order knowledge, and a manner of expressing or encoding it similar to our own, speculative work would have been unnecessary and the paradox of supposed primitives producing artistic major wonders would have never arisen.

Beyond a certain level, in every one of the arts and sciences of Egypt, knowledge was kept secret. The rules, axioms, theorems

---

[5] Malkowski, E.F. 2007. (p. 180)
[6] West, J.A. 1993. (p. 19)

5

and formulae- the very stuff of modern science and scholarship-were never made public, and may never have been written down.[7] In every field of Egyptian knowledge, the underlying principles were kept secret, but made manifest in works. That Egypt possessed this knowledge is incontestable in the face of the harmonic proportions of her art and architecture, as revealed by people such as Schwaller de Lubicz.[8]

René A. Schwaller de Lubicz (1887 – 1961), born in Alsace-Lorraine, was best known for his 15-year study of the art and architecture of the Temple of Luxor in Egypt and his subsequent book "The Temple of Man." He is known for his role in outlining what is known as sacred Egyptian architecture. His elucidation of the Temple of Luxor and his presentation of the Egyptian understanding of a special quality of innate consciousness form a bridge that attempts to link the sacred science of the Ancients to its modern rediscovery in our own time. In his chief work, The Temple of Man, he proposes, and argues in detail, for an interpretation of the Egyptian outlook rooted in numerology and sacred geometry, based on applied Pythagorean concepts.

The groundbreaking work of Schwaller De Lubicz brought new insight into contemporary understanding of the Pythagorean Number Mysticism and Symbolism. His work, especially at the Temple of Luxor, provided sufficient evidence for us to see how the Egyptians applied Pythagorean principles in practice. Here the essence relies on qualitative functionality, principle and process, rather than mere quantity and strict mathematical prescriptions. In addition, Egyptian society had profound and exact knowledge of the principles responsible for the created universe, which fits perfectly into the framework that the Pythagorean Number System provides. John Anthony West reasons that the Symbolist interpretation supports this claim with two kinds of evidence, i) linguistic, and ii) mathematical.

---

[7] West, J.A. 1993. (p. 24)
[8] West, J.A. 1993. (p. 24)

i) Linguistic

Though simple enough to explain and illustrate, the symbolic key to the hieroglyphs requires a kind of thinking that opposes the analytic and scientific spirit of modern day thought. In Egypt, the hieroglyph refers not only to the physical entity it represents, but also to all the functions and properties that are contained within the "idea" of the physical entity. It is as holistic as any form of communication can be. The failure to understand both the purpose of myth and its underlying truth contributes to the current unsatisfactory understanding of ancient Egypt. Myth expresses cosmic laws, principles, processes and functions, which in turn may be defined and described by number and the relationship between them.

ii) Mathematical

The deliberate presence of harmonic proportions in art and architecture, as well as the numerical basis underlying the Egyptian cosmology, compelled Schwaller de Lubicz to a detailed reconsideration of Pythagoreanism, and to the construction of a system of thought that explains the masterpieces of Egypt- with the fact of an empire that lasted four thousand years. However, our discursive language allows for no convenient explanation of this system. In fact, ancient Egyptian hieroglyphs represent more than just a language. It is at once philosophy, mathematics, mysticism and theology. To comprehend it rightly, no aspect of it should be studied without simultaneously taking into account everything it represents. In Egypt, the accomplished structures permitted- and indeed compelled- this complex understanding. However, in order to explain it or describe it satisfactorily in modern language, we must do it gradually. *"Number is All,"* declared the Pythagoreans. To us, it seems odd to classify numbers as "limited, unlimited, odd, even, single, multiple, left, right, male, female, rectangular, curved, light, dark, etc." It seems even more odd to call five the number of "love" and eight the number of "justice." Yet, it seems less odd once we consider the thinking that led to these attributions. [9]

A much stronger argument for the Egyptian origin of the Number System can be found when one grasps the fundamental principles of ancient Egyptian religion. The science of Numbers, measurements and proportions are the factors of universal Harmony. As geometry was the indispensable basis of Pythagorean initiation, this science was likely treated in Egypt as the operation of the forces and forms produced by the *movement* of Number, *'I am One which becomes two, I am Two which became Four....'* And this Number the manifest power of the highest Power *'whose name is hidden,'* is the unknowable Absolute shown in action throughout the whole Genesis as represented in the Egyptian creation myth. It is at work in the first duplication, Shu and Tefnut, issuing from the Primordial Source (or One). It is at work in all personifications in of the various aspects of the four elements. It is at work in the generative action of the Ennead; it is at work in all the multiplying divisions of the first maternal Neter, Apet, who 'numbers' by producing the procreative functions, and multiplies them with the function of 'nourishing.' It is at work in the operation of the goddess Sefekht (seven), who personifies the power of the septenary in the manifestation of the Energy on earth (seven colors in light, seven musical tones, etc.).[10] It is at work in the numbering of the geographical division of land, and succession of dynasties, whose numerical order so strangely

---

[9] West, J.A. 1993. (p. 30)
[10] Schwaller de Lubicz, I. 1978. (p. 329)

conforms to the evolutionary 'ages' or stages of Royal man, whose symbolic history is represented by the Pharaohs.[11]

The philosophy of number is based on the functional character of number.[12] Yet, modern thinking reduces number to the concept of "measure," that is, to a definition of "quantity." Contemporary science expects of us to quantify almost everything, even so the abstract. This removes the esoteric character of Number, which resides in the "function" that it reveals and not in the measure that it specifies or counts. We do not attribute the notion of division to the number Two. It is the number Two that implies the process of dualizing from which our understanding of division derives. It is therefore, antithetical to current belief. This phenomenon is not accidental. It is cosmic, the conscious revelation of our innate knowledge and therefore, represents a form of consciousness.[13] The Egyptians applied this knowledge when building their Temples and pyramids. Yet, the Egyptians were not supposed to have understood the laws of harmony and proportion by then, or have known of the existence of irrationals, as they were supposedly Greek inventions of a much later time in history. [14]

The Temple of Luxor, which Schwaller de Lubicz calls "The Temple of Man," is the perfect practical example of this symbolic understanding in action.[15] It is a vast stone symbol, the greatest achievement of New Kingdom Egypt, incorporating within it- or utilizing- the totality of Egyptian wisdom, science, mathematics, geodesy, geography, geometry, medicine, astronomy, astrology, magic, myth, art, and symbolism. It is upon the knowledge of functional identity- the philosophy of

---

[11] Schwaller de Lubicz, I. 1978. (p. 329)
[12] Schwaller de Lubicz, R.A. 1998.
[13] West, J.A. 1993. (p. 30)
[14] West, J.A. 1993. (p. 21)
[15] West, J.A. 1993. (p. 152)

the Unity- that the magic of religious rituals, the liturgy, and the perfect architecture of this temple is established. [16]

A lifetime's study of mathematics- and particularly the mathematics of number, harmony and proportion- had convinced Schwaller de Lubicz that however distorted and diffuse the teachings of Pythagoras had become, in their pure form, they held the key to this ultimate mystery.[17] Schwaller de Lubicz dedicated his life towards proving this, spending 15 years at the site of the Temple, taking measurements by the inch. The Temple of Luxor tells, in stone, in its proportions and harmonies, its art and sculpture, the story of the creation of man; it signals his development, stage by stage, and it recreates in artistic form man's relationship to the universe.[18] In essence, the Temple of Luxor is designed to evoke understanding of the creative power of the Absolute through a strict imitation of its creative processes. It is examples such as these, which force us to believe that the ancient Egyptian civilization possessed Pythagorean knowledge.

The Greek Origin

We believe that Pythagoras (570-500 BCE) introduced the logic of the Number System into Western civilization. It is in this form that it is still in use today. Pythagoras was, in the Platonic-Plotinian tradition, an archetype of the Sage.[19] In fact, some authors held Pythagoras in such high regard, that they equate him with the figure of Christ.

It is uncertain exactly where Pythagoras gained his inspiration from, but what we do know is that he spent most of his life in the presence of priests and philosophers, that mentored him. It

---

[16] Schwaller de Lubicz, R.A. 1998. (Volume II, plate 77)
[17] West, J.A. 1993. (p. 22)
[18] West, J.A. 1993. (p. 153)
[19] Dillon, J. and Hershbell, J. 1991. (p. 14)

is suggested that Pythagoras borrowed the Number System from the Egyptians, while he was in Egypt for his own training as a priest, but even this is not known as fact. Iamblichus suggested that Pythagoras spent twenty-two years in Egypt. Egypt, at the time of Pythagoras, was already two thousand years old and a well-known center for learning during ancient times. Yet, other sources also suggest that Pythagoras discovered this science by himself, rather through the art of music and personal observation.[20] By then, Pythagoras was already known for his knowledge of harmony and harmonic ratios and even applied what he called "medical treatment through music" to "manipulate" crowds of people.[21] Notwithstanding, on his return from Egypt, Pythagoras found the Pythagorean Brotherhood to apply his mathematical, philosophical and harmonic theories to the moral and practical spheres of everyday life. Within decades, it dissolved, but small groups of isolated individuals continued to regard themselves as Pythagoreans.[22] What Pythagoras did establish, was a fundamental characterization and description of nature translated in numbers.

In the same era as Pythagoras, another philosopher, Empedocles, manifested strong Pythagorean principles in his philosophy. Empedocles was from the Greek colony Acragas-modern Agrigento- on the south-west coast of Sicily. Formulated in terms of the later trend defining separate fields of interest or expertise, his influence made itself felt in philosophy, rhetoric, medicine, chemistry, biology, astronomy, cosmology, psychology, mysticism, and religion. The immensely influential theory of four elements, first presented in western literature by Empedocles, is just one obvious example of his influence.[23] Empedocles used poetry to communicate his teaching, which unfortunately only survived in the form of

[20] Malkowski, E.F. 2007. (p. 165)
[21] Dillon, J. and Hershbell, J. 1991. (p. 135)
[22] West, J.A. 1993. (p. 19)
[23] Kingsley, P. 1995. (Introduction)

fragments that appeared in the texts of later writers. The work of Empedocles is significant in that it shows a broadly cyclical pattern, with elements of Empedoclean and Pythagorean doctrine deriving from near Eastern sources and in the course of centuries, making their way back to the East.[24] The work of Empedocles contains elements derived from Italian of Sicilian Pythagoreanism, which also later showed up in Plato's work. Plato's mythical geography- in particular his intricate picture of Tartarus and the great fires inside the earth- came to him from western Pythagoreans in the like of Empedocles.[25] Empedocles may not have written any valuable work pertaining to the Number System itself, but it is suggested that the influence of his work helped shape Neoplatonic thought.

A number of Greek philosophers, of whom Plato, Aristotle and Iamblichus, as well as a number of Greek writers also known as the Doxographists, later based their own philosophy mainly on that of Pythagoras, also incorporating elements of other individuals, such as Empedocles, and the Egyptians. In fact, there exists a strong association between Platonic and Pythagorean ideas, to the extent that Aristotle couples Pythagoreans with Platonists, and turns from describing Pythagorean ideas to outline Platonic ones.[26] In his mind, this was no arbitrary procedure, but reflected his perception of the extent to which Platonism was historically indebted to Pythagoreanism.[27] Key to this philosophy was the idea that there is unity in multiplicity, the concept of the One evolving and pervading the many.[28] At the heart of Pythagoras's science was the belief that all relationships could be reduced to number associations, and that all things are in fact numbers. Pythagoras himself said "All things are like unto number." [29]

[24] Kingsley, P. 1995. (Introduction)
[25] Kingsley, P. 1995. (p. 93)
[26] Kingsley, P. 1995. (p. 177)
[27] Kingsley, P. 1995. (p. 177)
[28] Malkowski, E.F. 2007. (p. 164)
[29] Delatte, A. 1915.

Iamblichus (245-325), also known as Iamblichus Chalcidensis, was an Assyrian Neoplatonist, Theurgist and philosopher who determined the direction taken by later Neoplatonic philosophy, and perhaps western Paganism itself. Iamblichus initially studied under Anatolius of Laodicea, and later went on to study under Porphyry, a pupil of Plotinus, the founder of Neoplatonism. *The Six Enneads*, sometimes abbreviated to *The Enneads* or *Enneads*, is the collection of writings of Plotinus, edited and compiled by his student Porphyry (circa 270 CE). His work, through Augustine of Hippo, and therefore subsequent Christian and Muslim thinkers, has greatly influenced Western and Near-Eastern thought.

Plotinus denied that the human soul completely descends into a body. The undescended soul of Plotinus exhibits the same traits and is described with the same metaphors as the Gnostics' Sophia. Plotinus himself admitted that his view was unorthodox and it was condemned by nearly all post-Iamblichean Platonists. The problem Plotinus was attempting to solve with this doctrine of the undescended soul was how to account for the soul's suffering and experience of evil.[30] Iamblichus apposed this view with his belief in an embodied soul.

Plotinus and his student Porphyry were therefore, camped together against Iamblichus, even though all of them were outspokenly Pythagorean. It was with Porphyry that Iamblichus is also known to have had a disagreement over the practice of Theurgy. Porphyry believed that mental contemplation alone could bring salvation. He had challenged the authenticity of Theurgic divination. In his letter to Anebo, Porphyry implied that Theurgic rites attempted to manipulate the gods and that Theurgists stood on magical characters to impose their will on the gods.[31] For Iamblichus, the deification of the soul could not be effected by introspection because the embodied soul had no immediate access to the divine. In light of this, Iamblichus

---

[30] Shaw, G. 1951. (p. 65)
[31] Shaw, G. 1951. (p. 85)

developed a soteriological practice that by its very name, *theourgia*, defines not what the soul does, but what gods do through the soul.

In *"Theurgy"* or *"On the Mysteries of Egypt"* Iamblichus expounded on his Egyptian beliefs and traditions, which included the practice of Theurgy. The differences between this book and Iamblichus' other works in style and in some points of doctrine have led some to question whether Iamblichus was the actual author. Yet, some sources do argue that Iamblichus believed that the Egyptian cosmology was based on such a strong foundation that it could be used as a proxy to convince his Greek counterparts to accept his view. Still, there is no doubt that the treatise *"On the Mysteries of Egypt"* certainly originated from his school, and in its systematic attempt to give a speculative justification of the polytheistic cult practices of the day, it marks a turning point in the history of thought where Iamblichus stood. This text is still in print today.

Iamblichus' analysis was that the transcendent could not be grasped with mental contemplation because the transcendent is supra rational (based on or involving factors not to be comprehended by reason alone). With Iamblichus and his advocacy of Theurgy as a necessary complement to theology, Dillon and Hershbell reasons that Platonism also becomes more explicitly a religion.[32] This is not entirely true. The addition of Theurgy provides the individual with an opportunity to approach Platonism as a religion. The system fits perfectly well into the realm of both the theistic and non-theistic practice of the Left-Hand Path.

Nevertheless, the addition of magic introduced a new element to Platonism. Iamblichus therefore, draws attention to Pythagoreanism as the *"divine philosophy."*[33] It is with this aspect of Iamblichus, and his *"The Theology of Arithmetic,"* where our further interest lies. Here Iamblichus provides a

---

[32] Dillon, J. and Hershbell, J. 1991. (p. 18)
[33] Dillon, J. and Hershbell, J. 1991. (p. 1)

concise summary of the philosophy of the Pythagorean Number System. This system itself is still in use today. The *"Ceremony of the Nine Angles,"* published in *"The Satanic Rituals"* is an excellent example of such. The *"Theology of Arithmetic"* as it has been transmitted, is largely a cento of passages from lost work of Nicomachus of Gerasa (by the same title) and one of Anatolius, presumably Iamblichus' teacher, *"On the Decade and the Numbers Within It."*

Iamblichus' statements in the *"De Vita Pythagorica"* that understanding the "nobility and greatness" of Pythagoras's philosophy, is a very slow process, and that the god's assistance is necessary, is much influenced by the writings of Plato, in *Timaues 27c*. It is important to note that Iamblichus believed that those who distanced themselves from his view also distanced themselves from the essence of true Platonic principles. The *"De Vita Pythagorica"* is a very important work for the history of the Pythagoras legend, and for understanding Iamblichus' own Platonic beliefs in which philosophy and religion were closely connected. This serves as an additional justification to believe that there exist a close connection between Platonism and Pythagoreanism, which even today, still exists. Plato himself believed in the esoteric use of Numbers. In *"De Vita Pythagorica"* Iamblichus wrote that Plato believed the study of Numbers awakens an organ in the brain, which the ancients described as "the third eye" or "eye of wisdom," now known to physiology as the pineal gland. Plato (in *The Republic Book VII*) also insisted that the science of numbers was not to be used for mere buying and selling, but *'to help in the conversion of the soul itself from the world of becoming to truth and reality.'*

Iamblichus was highly praised by those who followed his thought. His contemporaries accredited Iamblichus with miraculous powers. The Roman emperor Julian regarded Iamblichus as more than second to Plato. During the revival of interest in his philosophy in the 15th and 16th centuries, the name of Iamblichus was scarcely mentioned without the epithet "divine" or "most divine." Unfortunately, only a few books of Iamblichus survived, most of them having been destroyed during the Christianization of the Roman Empire.

"We know infinitesimally little of the material Universe. Our detailed knowledge is so contemptibly minute, that it is hardly worth reference, save that our shame may spur us to increased endeavor. Such knowledge as we have got is of a very general and abstruse, of a philosophical and almost magical character. This consists principally of the conceptions of pure mathematics. It is, therefore, almost legitimate to say that pure mathematics is our link with the rest of the Universe and with "God."

-Aleister Crowley-

Pythagoras' Cosmology

With the emergence of the Greek educational system after the fifth century BCE, Pythagorean concepts helped inspire a new generation of philosophers. With the works of Socrates, Plato and Aristotle, a completely new world was born, a world that eventually became Western civilization. Thus, for many scholars the "Greek Miracle" is the starting point, the beginning of philosophy and science.[34] Yet, it is important to bear in mind that there does not appear to be such a thing as one orthodox position to which all Pythagoreans adhere.[35]

Pythagoras held that one of the first principles, the Monad, is god and the good, which is the origin of the One, and is itself intelligence; but the undefined Dyad (Two) is a divinity and the bad surrounding which is the mass of matter. Divine spirits are psychical beings; and heroes are souls separated from bodies, good heroes are good souls, bad heroes are bad souls. The followers of Thales and Pythagoras and the Stoics held that matter is variable and changeable and transformable and in a

---

[34] Malkowski, E.F. 2007. (p.193)
[35] Kingsley, P. 1995. (p.182)

17

state of flux. Pythagoras asserted that the so-called forms and ideas exist in numbers and their harmonies, and in what are called geometrical objects, apart from bodies. Pythagoras and Aristotle asserted that the first causes are immaterial, but that other causes involve a union or contact with material substance [so that the world is material]. Bodies are subject to change of condition, and are divisible to infinity.

Pythagoras believed that "Deity geometrizes," meaning that physical forms in the universe are created in an outward fashion from within. When numbers represents digits, they are symbolic of a quantity. In Pythagorean philosophy, they represent entities that are symbolic of the nature and origin of the universe. Pythagoras also discovered that there are only five symmetrical solids- the tetrahedron (four equilateral triangles), cube (six squares), octahedron (eight equilateral triangles), icosahedrons (twenty equilateral triangles), and dodecahedron (twelve regular pentagons). All matter (the four elements) was believed to be composed of the symmetrical solids- earth was cubical, fire tetrahedral, water icosahedral and air, octahedral.

A face requires at least three sides, so the first Pythagorean number in form is Three (the surface), representing the Triangle. The second number is Four (the solid), representing the Square. One (the dot) and Two (the line), not being numbers in form, symbolize the two abstract spheres of existence, the Supreme World and the Superior World, reserved for principles and intelligences. The Supreme World is the arena of the divine. In it is the essence of the universe and all that the universe comprises. Within the Superior World, the home of the immortals, exists all archetypes that provide the symbolic imagery for the material world. The material World is, of course, the immediate, observable world. Earlier cosmologies had, as a matter of course, placed the earth at the centre of the Universe. However, later in time this system gives the central place to a fiery "hearth" (or "central fire"), surrounded by a number of bodies revolving around it in circular orbits at various different distances from it; and one of those revolving bodies is our earth.[36]

Even though the world of Pythagoras seems abstract and derived from Number, it is clear from existing literature that he did own a formal cosmological identity, in which gods that are more specific, played a central role. The details of his cosmology are not known. Yet, is reported that when Epimenedes, a disciple of Pythagoras, was about to be killed by certain persons, Pythagoras invoked the Erinyes and the avenging gods, and caused those plotting against him to kill one another all at once, or so it would seem. Pythagoras also, coming to aid human beings, punished and delivered up to death him who committed violence and crimes against humanity. He did this by means of Apollo's oracles with which he was naturally joined together from his birth. [37]

Neoplatonic Cosmology

Perhaps the greatest single contribution the Greeks made to subsequent Jewish, Islamic and Christian thought was through their conception of Creation as emanation. Our focus lies only with the cosmologies of those individuals that identified themselves as both Neoplatonists and Pythagoreans.

We can reduce Neoplatonic Pythagorean cosmology to two schools of thought- those who supported the practice of magic or Theurgy (Iamblichus) and those that opposed the use of magic or Theurgy (Plotinus and Porphyry) as a complement to philosophy. Even though the basic structure of their cosmologies is very similar, there exist philosophical differences that affect the way it is approached in practice. Furthermore, it is important to acknowledge that the Pythagorean movement

---

[36] Kingsley, P. 1995 (p. 172)
[37] Dillon, J. and Hershbell, J. 1991. (p. 222)

never prescribed the specific contents of an individual cosmology, but rather provides the basic framework within which the individual himself applies his or her own cosmology. We, therefore, deal here with Neoplatonic cosmology applied to the Pythagorean framework. [Neo-]Platonism itself is a cosmology or a worldview. It is also, simultaneously, a cosmogony, or an explanation of how the universe (or cosmos) comes into being, and how it is sustained. It is also important that we recognize that the selected sections that follow form only a small part of a more comprehensive system of emanations used to explain the origin of both the material and immaterial universe. In this system in every order of things, a triad is the immediate progeny of a monad. Hence, the intelligible triad proceeds immediately from the ineffable principle of things (The Monad, Absolute, or One). Phanes, also known as Protogonos, or intelligible intellect, who is the last of the intelligible order, is the monad, leader, and producing cause of a new triad, which is known as *intelligible, and at the same time intellectual*. In like manner, the extremity of this triad produces immediately from itself the intellectual triad (Saturn, Rhea and Jupiter). Jupiter represents what is generally known as the Demiurge* [in Neoplatonic philosophy the Demiurge also represents the nous; Zeus in Greek mythology], responsible for the creation of the physical universe, who also becomes the Monad of the supermundane triad. Apollo, who subsists at the

---

*Demiurge: Gnosticism also presents a distinction between the highest, unknowable God and the demiurgic "creator" of the material. In contrast to Plato, several systems of Gnostic thought present the Demiurge as antagonistic to the will of the Supreme Being: his act of creation occurs in unconscious semblance of the divine model, and thus is fundamentally flawed, or else is formed with the malevolent intention of entrapping aspects of the divine *in* materiality. Thus, in such systems, the demiurge acts as a solution to the problem of evil. In the *Apocryphon of John* circa 200 AD, the demiurge has the name "Yaldabaoth," and proclaims himself as God: "Now the archon (ruler) who is weak has three names. The first name is Yaltabaoth, the second

extremity of the supermundane order, produces a triad of liberated gods. In addition, the extremity of the liberated gods becomes the Monad of a triad of mundane gods.

All beings therefore, proceed from, and are comprehended in, the First Being: all intellects emanate from one First Intellect; all souls from one First Soul; all natures blossom from one First Nature; and all bodies proceed from the vital and luminous body of the world. [38] All these great monads are comprehended in the first One, from which both they and all their depending series are unfolded into light. Hence, the First One is truly the unity of unities, the Monad of Monads, the principle of principles, the God of Gods, One and all things, and yet, One prior to All.

"You will see one according law and assertion in all the earth, that there is one God, the king and father of all things, and many Gods, sons of God, ruling together with him."

-Maximus Tyruis-

---

is Saklas ("fool"), and the third is Samael. And he is impious in his arrogance which is in him. For he said, 'I am God and there is no other God beside me,' for he is ignorant of his strength, the place from which he had come." Still others equated the Demiurge with Satan. Catharism apparently inherited their idea of Satan as the creator of the evil world directly or indirectly from Gnosticism. "The god of this world" is mentioned by Paul in 2 Corinthians 4:4; John states that "the whole world lies in the grip of the Wicked One" (1 John 5:19). While the Gnostics saw this as a reference to the Demiurge (and, by association, to Satan), this vilification of the Creator of the material world was inimical to both orthodox Christianity and orthodox Judaism.

---

[38] Iamblichus (2006 translation). (p. xiii)

The basic Neoplatonic cosmogony and cosmology, shows a threefold emanation to man.[39] For Plotinus and Iamblichus' teachers Anatolius and Porphyry, the emanations were as follows:

- To En (τό ἕν), The One: Deity without quality, also called The Good*;
- Nous (Νοῦς), Mind: The Universal Soul or consciousness, from which proceeds;
- Psychè (Ψυχή), Soul: Including both Individual and World-Soul, leading finally to
- Physis (Φύσις), Nature.

Each level of emanation was called a hypostasis. Each hypostasis, or emanation, caused the next lower one. As the emanations proceeded from one to the other, they got more and more physical. First, The One emanated into the hypostasis of The Intellect, The Intellect then emanated outwards and downwards into the Universal Soul, the Universal Soul into Individual Souls; and the Individual Souls into individual personalities of both humans and animals, each with its physical body.

The One is the origin of all things, equated with God. God created as an intermediary the "maker"- the *demiourgos* (demiurge or *nous*) also called the Word (Logos), which is a perfect image of the One and the archetype of all existing things. It is at once being and thought, ideal world and idea. As image, the *nous* corresponds perfectly to the One, but as

---

*The Good: Iamblichus distinguishes between two types of Good- the good itself which is beyond essence, and there is that good which subsists according to essence.

---

[39] Flowers, S.E. 1995. (p. 51)

derived it is entirely different. What Plotinus understands by the *nous* is the highest sphere accessible to the human *mind*, and, along with that, pure *intellect* itself. The demiurge or nous is the energy or ergon (does the work) that manifests or organizes the material world into perceivability.

The creation of the Word is called the All- or World-Soul, which, according to Plotinus, is, like the *nous*, immaterial. The Word is the active agent of divine creation, while the All-Soul is the very plan or blueprint of manifestation. Its relation to the *nous* is the same as that of the *nous* to the One. It stands between the *nous* and the phenomenal world, is permeated and illuminated by the former, but is also in contact with the latter. The *nous* is indivisible; the World-Soul may preserve its unity and remain in the *nous*, but at the same time it has the power of uniting with the corporeal world and thus being disintegrated. It therefore occupies an intermediate position. As a single World-Soul it belongs in essence and destination to the intelligible world; but it also embraces innumerable Individual Souls; and these can either submit to be ruled by the *nous*, or turn aside from the intellect and choose the sensual and lose themselves in the finite.

All three members of the triad are but three parts of the Divine. The first part is the One (Monad), the First Existent, also called the Good (*agathon*) or sometimes "the Father." The second part is the First Thinker and the First Thought- the vision of the Divine. This is the Maker, often called the "Son of God." Part three is the expression of the outgoing activity or *energy* of the Divine. It becomes the basis for material manifestation.

In Neoplatonic thought the essence of being is the equivalent of its characteristic action- Love is the equivalent of Loving, for the relative Being of Love can have no other action than *to Love*. In addition, each entity in the chain of Being is a reflection, or "shadow," of that which is above it, or from which it emanated. It then both contemplates and aspires toward that which generated it, and in turn also generates and image of itself below itself. And so the chain of Being goes until its energy ebbs and it finally ceases. Being is seen to be analogues to a light shining into darkness- the light is strongest where it is closest to its source, the further it is from its source, the more diffuse it is. Matter arises at that point where the creative power of the All Soul comes to an end. Matter is almost non-Being, as a mixture being between Being and non-being. Absolute non-Being cannot, strictly speaking, exist in a cosmos that emanates from the fullness of being.[40] The supernal triad of the One-Divine Mind-All-Soul reflects itself continually in levels below, or "after" it.

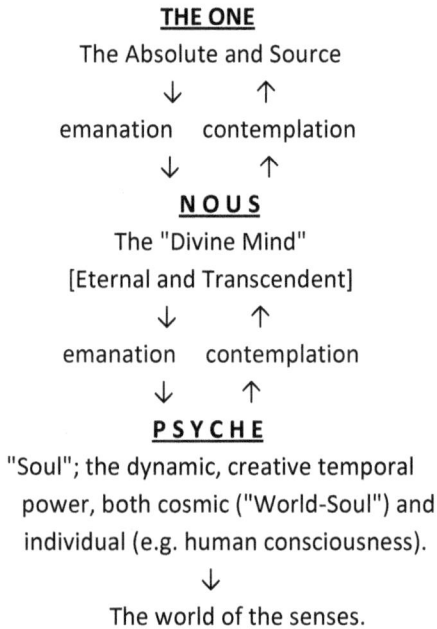

THE ONE

The Absolute and Source

↓   ↑

emanation   contemplation

↓   ↑

N O U S

The "Divine Mind"

[Eternal and Transcendent]

↓   ↑

emanation   contemplation

↓   ↑

P S Y C H E

"Soul"; the dynamic, creative temporal

power, both cosmic ("World-Soul") and

individual (e.g. human consciousness).

↓

The world of the senses.

Plotinus distinguishes two stages of emanation. The first, *prohodros* or Procession is the formless, infinite stream of life that flows forth from the One. However, it is impossible for

---

[40] Flowers, S.E. 1995. (p. 52)

beings to receive any shape as long as the descent into multiplicity continues unchecked; they must turn back upon themselves and imitate the perfection of their Origin to the best of their ability. Hence, in the second stage, *epistrophe*, Reversion, being turns back, contemplates the One, and so receives form and order. In the subdivision of the second hypostasis into Being, Intelligence, and Life, Life the Second Hypostasis in its unformed stage, Procession, and Intelligence to the second stage, Reversion, when it has received form and limit.

As mentioned earlier, Plotinus believed that the World-Soul does not fall and neither do Individual Souls. The suffering of Individual Souls, therefore, is merely the suffering of their "images"; in truth, Individual Souls remain above, at the level of the World-Soul. In his view, the World-Soul is equal to the unfallen Individual Souls. [41]

Iamblichus, as a Theurgist under the influence of Pythagorean arithmology, viewed all manifestation, sensible or intelligible, as reducible to numerical principles, and it is possible that many important differences between pre- and post-Iamblicheans were due more to the influence on Iamblichus of an "immanentist" Pythagorean metaphysics than to his reputed "Oriental" predisposition to "alien ideas." [42]

Iamblichus believed that the God, or Platonic Demiurge, is not the creator of matter, but when he receives it, as eternal, he molds it into forms and organizes it according to numerical ratios. In *De Mysteriis,* Iamblichus describes the Demiurge as the paternal Monad (itself derived from a higher unity) that gave rise to the division of materiality and substantiality. The consistency of Iamblichus's metaphysics is borne out of Damascius, who said that Iamblichus asserted an "entirely ineffable" One (*pantelōs arrheton*) prior to the simple unity (*ho haplōs hen*) that preceded the limit (*peras*) and unlimited

---

[41] Shaw, G. 1951. (p. 65)
[42] Shaw, G. 1951. (p. 30)

(*apeiron*) and whose mixing gave rise to the One-Being (*to hen on*). The dyad, Iamblichus said more specifically, served as a borderland (*metaichmion*) between the multiple *arithmoi*, represented by the triad, and the monad. He therefore, considered the monad as "mother of all numbers" and served as the matrix that transformed the monad into *arithmoi*.[43] In his view form and matter in the cosmos are analogues to the monad and dyad in numbers, and maintained that just as numbers are derived from combinations of the monad and dyad, the manifest world is derived from a demiurge activity that he called the "rhythmic weaving" of monadic and dyadic archai. If the Many is conceived as a Triad and that opposed to the Many is conceived as a Monad, the Dyad would be a borderland between them. Therefore, the Dyad possesses the characteristics of both. Arithmogony, for Iamblichus, was the analogue of cosmogony, and both expressed the harmony of opposed principles. There is nothing in existence in which opposition is not present. These oppositions, held in measured grades of tension and proportion, made up the framework for physical manifestation.

Iamblichus's celestial gods (souls) mediate between the World-Soul and Individual Souls. Like the Dyad in the mathematical example, celestial gods are the borderland (*metachmion*) between the exempt wholeness and unity of the World-Soul and the multiplicity and division of Individual Souls. Celestial souls possess the characteristics of their extremes: they never depart from their pure condition, but like Individual Souls, they each possess a single and moving body.[44] Indeed, what distinguished the Theurgical Platonism of Iamblichus from the "exalted soul" Platonism of Plotinus was their interpretations of how the soul attained its celestial identity. The angelic soul of the Theurgist was the functional equivalent of Plotinus's undescended soul, yet the two Platonists in strongly contrasting terms explained the realization of this divine status. For

---

[43] Shaw, G. 1951. (p. 34)
[44] Shaw, G. 1951. (p. 67)

Iamblichus the Theurgist attained this rank through ritual practices and a demiurge assimilation of all the powers that he encountered in embodiment. For Plotinus, it was less an assimilation of cosmic powers than a realization that the soul, as undescended, somehow never really encountered them.

Iamblichus's Theurgical Platonism was "locative" in a highly sophisticated way. In both traditional and Theurgical Platonism, the daemonic was not an external evil on the fringe of the cosmos, for the cosmos was all embracing and entirely good. Iamblichus, like Plato, placed the daemonic within the embodied soul, the only chaos untamed by the Demiurge. [45]

While Plato's Demiurge gave to each soul a spark of himself, Iamblichus understood this to mean that each soul had the responsibility to perform its own demiurgy, that is to say, its own Theurgy. The task for every soul was to partake in divine mimesis by creating a cosmos out of the initial chaos of its embodiment. Therefore, the "daemonic" condition of the embodied soul was a *felix culpa* without which the soul could not participate in cosmogenesis, including its own creation and salvation. For Iamblichus, the cosmos itself was the paradigmatic Theurgy: the act of the gods continually extending themselves into mortal expression.[46] In Platonic terms, this meant taking an active part in the demiurgy of the cosmos and becoming co-creator with the god of creation. Iamblichus turned to the Egyptians to explain this phenomenon. The Egyptians praised by Iamblichus worshipped the true gods of Platonism: the unchanging patterns of nature; they were a community perfectly integrated with the natural world, reproducing in cult and ritual activity of the demiurge in the cosmos. [47] Iamblichus saw the embodiment of the soul and its perfection in Theurgy as essential to cosmogenesis.

---

[45] Shaw, G. 1951. (p. 15)
[46] Shaw, G. 1951. (p. 17)
[47] Shaw, G. 1951. (p. 23)

Ancient Egyptian Cosmology

"Ancient Egypt always saw the cause through the effect. Indeed, this was the essential characteristic of the Egyptian method: observation of the concrete fact or the concrete symbol of a fact, for the purpose of rousing in the student the evocation of its abstract aspects."

-Isha Schwaller de Lubicz-

The word Egypt can be derived from the Greek word *Aigyptos*, a transcription of *Haikuptah*- Ha-Ka-Ptah- the name of Ptah's temple at Memphis.[48] In the Egyptian texts Egypt was known by several names, of which our main concern lies with *Ta nutria*, the *'land of the Neters,'* or *'land of the Gods.'* In general, it was believed that Egypt was organized in the Image of the Heaven:

"O Asclepius, that Egypt is the copy of Heaven, or rather, the place where here below are mediated and projected all operations which govern and actuate the heavenly forces? Even more than that, if the whole truth is to be told, our land is the temple of the entire World."

-Hermes Trismegistus to Asclepius-

The names and towns of Egypt were determined by the fundamental characteristic of each place; there is therefore a relation between them and the symbolism of the different geographical locations, since each geographical location geographic location corresponds to one organic function in the body of Egypt, which claims to be organized in the image of Heaven.[49]

---

[48] Schwaller de Lubicz, I. 1978. (p. 305)
[49] Schwaller de Lubicz, I. 1978. (p. 307)

For the Egyptians, the biggest mystery of all was the "becoming" of the creator from the unseen into the seen, the One who manifests as many.[50] This becoming was manifest through four successive stages which were represented by the major Temples: Atum-Râ as the primordial creation taught at Heliopolis, Ptah as its realization at Memphis, Thoth as its theory of genesis at Hermopolis, and Amun as its achievement at Thebes. Temples were conceived as the seats of the Neters, each a dwelling place of the particular Principle to which each of them was dedicated. The study of the primary and secondary Cause follows naturally from this Cosmogony and constitutes the whole history of the Neters, which is the Egyptian theogony-theology. Egyptian wisdom thought of Heaven as the seat of the Neters, that is to say, the creative Causes or agents of continuous creation and the principles of Functions which through reflection into the earthly world maintained its existence. [51]

According to the Leyden Papyrus of Qenna, written during the Twenty-Eighth Dynasty:

"All gods are three: Amun, Re, and Ptah, who have no equals. He whose nature is mysterious, being Amun; Ra is the head, Ptah is the body. Their cities on Earth, established forever are: Thebes, Heliopolis, and Memphis for eternity. When a message comes from heaven, it is heard at Heliopolis, it is repeated at Memphis to Ptah, and it is made into a letter written in the letters of Thoth [at Hermopolis] for the city of Amun [Thales]."

This idea of a message represents the progress of the "becoming" from heaven to earth. Heliopolis was considered the "ear of the heart," or city of the sun. In the beginning of the beginning there was the Primordial Chaos, Nun. From this chaos, by his own power, rose the Sun (Atum-Râ, he who

---

[50] Malkowski, E.F. 2007. (p. 184)
[51] Schwaller de Lubicz, I. 1978. (p. 329)

creates himself). His name is thought to be derived from the word 'tem', which means to complete or finish. Thus, he has been interpreted as being the 'complete one' and the finisher of the world, which he returns to watery chaos at the end of the creative cycle. As creator he was seen as the underlying substance of the world, the deities and all things being made of his flesh or alternatively being his ka.

The sun was considered the heart of the solar system. Heliopolis therefore, also means the "absolute origin of all things." Atum-Râ, masturbating and spitting, produced Shu (air/wind- life) and Tefnut (water/ moisture- order), introducing social order. Shu and Tefnut produced Geb (Earth) and Nut (Sky). When Geb and Nut meet, Darkness occurs. Geb and Nut gave birth to Osiris, Isis, Set and Nepthys. Together they are known as the Great Ennead (or nine great Osirian gods) of Heliopolis. Osiris, Isis, Set and Nepthys represent the cyclical nature of life, death and rebirth. In applying the four principles (unity, duality, reconciliation and the concept of matter), Osiris represents incarnation and reincarnation, life and death, which is renewal. Isis is the feminine aspect of Osiris. Set is the principle of opposition, or antagonism, and Nephthys, the feminine aspect of Set. What is really being dealt with here is the primordial mystery of God and His creation, Atum-Râ, who becomes One, then Two, and so on up to Eight:

> *'I am one that transforms into Two*
> *I am Two that transforms into Four*
> *I am Four that transforms into Eight*
> *After this I am One'*
> -Coffin of Petamon, Cairo Musem-
> [Artifact number 116023]

John Anthony West reasons that the Great Ennead emanates from the Absolute or "central fire" (in the terminology of

Pythagoras).[52] The nine neters (or principles) are bounded by the One (the Absolute), which becomes both One and Ten, and is the symbolic likeness of the original unity. The neters can be categorized as metaphysical, cosmic and natural. To know the name of the neters means to know its particular activity, because the neter is a functional principle and not a god, as popular custom would have it.[53] With regards to the neters, Iamblichus remarks the following:

"I am that same God, the Supreme One, who has myriad of mysterious names." [54]

At Memphis, Ptah carries this abstraction further and brings down fire from heaven. In the Shabaka Stone it was stated that Ptah called the world into being, having dreamt creation in his heart and speaking it- his name meaning *opener*, in the sense of *opener of the mouth*. Indeed the *opening of the mouth* ceremony, performed by priests at funerals to release souls from their corpses, was said to have been created by Ptah. Ptah is perceived as the creator of everything on earth and the gods and goddesses who are his thoughts, go to form the elements of nature and the cosmic forces that maintain nature.

At Hermopolis the divine fire begins to interact with the other elements (water, air, earth and fire) within the terrestrial world. Eight primordial Neters are formed, represented in the shape of frogs and snakes. Between them these four couples create an egg which they deposit on the 'hill' risen from the Nun. From this egg is born the Sun.

At Thebes, a reiteration of these three processes is combined into one, represented by the triad of Amun. The eight primordial Neters (the Ogdoad) are carried by the waters from

---

[52] West, J.A. 1993. (p. 55)
[53] Malkowski, E.F. 2007. (p. 188)
[54] Iamblichus, 2006 translation. (p.326)

the Thebes to Hermopolis; there they create the Sun, after they return to die near the Theban Mountains. The dominant principle of the Theban theme is Amun, who is presented in three forms:

1. Kematef, "the one who has made his Time," a snake god;
2. Irta, "who makes the Earth," a second snake god succeeds to his father Kematef;
3. Amun, the member of the Ogdoad.

"Amun, creative Verb, ternary Unity, Amun, the unknowable,
He makes Eternity by closing the ring of Becoming and Return,
He makes Existence,
He who is Being, the Being who animates, Father of the Neters,
He is in the nourishing Water of things,
He is that which in things receives nourishment.
All that exists is from Amun, all is offered to Him.
He appears in Horakhty who opens the doors of Knowledge,
The colors Black and Green and White and Red are of Amun,
Master of the Four Winds.
Amun is the life of the ocean waters of the ocean, Nun.
He, the imponderable, contracts himself into that, which is weight,
Amun, the unknowable, is seed and matrix of all things."

-Inspired by the litanies to Amun carved on the east wall of the court of Ramesses in the Temple of Luxor-

Amun, reconstructed Egyptian *Yamānu* (also spelled *Amon*, *Amoun*, *Amen*) the focus of the most complex system of theology in Ancient Egypt. Whilst remaining hypostatic deities, Amun represented the essential and hidden. As the creator deity "par excellence," he was the champion of the poor and central to personal piety. Amun is considered to represent the Egyptian version of the Greek demiurge, who is the curator of truth and wisdom, descending into generation, and leading the power of occult reasons into light.

Amun was self-created, without mother and father, and during the New Kingdom, he became the greatest expression of transcendental deity in Egyptian theology. He was not considered imminent within creation nor was creation seen as an extension of himself. Amun, likewise with the Hebrew creator deity, did not physically engender the universe. His position as King of Gods developed to the point of virtual monotheism where other Gods became manifestations of him. With Osiris, Amun-Ra is the most widely recorded of the Egyptian Gods. According to legend, Amun created an Ogdoad (Eight) of other deities. The eight deities were arranged in four female-male pairs, the females were associated with snakes and the males were associated with frogs: Naunet and Nu, Amaunet and Amun, Kauket and Kuk, Huh and Hauhet. Apart from their gender, there was little to distinguish the female goddess from the male god in a pair; indeed, the names of the females are merely the female forms of the male name and vice versa. Essentially, each pair represents the female and male aspect of one of four concepts, namely the primordial waters (Naunet and Nu), air or invisibility (Amunet and Amun), darkness (Kauket and Kuk), and eternity or infinite space (Hauhet and Huh).

Together the four concepts represent the primal, fundamental state of the beginning- they are what always were. In the myth, however, their interaction ultimately proved to be unbalanced, resulting in the arising of a new entity. When the entity opened, it revealed Ra, the fiery sun, inside. After a long interval of rest, Ra, together with the other deities, created all other things.

Thus, the doctrine of the Egyptians concerning principles, proceeding from on high as far as to the last of things, begins from one principle, and descends to a multitude which is governed by this One; and everywhere an indefinite nature is under the dominion of a certain definite measure, and of the supreme uncial cause of all things. [55]

The goal of the Neterian disciplines is to discover the meaning of "Who am I?," to unravel the mysteries of life and to fathom the depths of eternity and infinity. This is the task of all human beings and it is to be accomplished in this very lifetime. This can be done by learning the ways of the Neteru, emulating them and finally becoming like them, Akhus (enlightened beings), walking the earth as giants and accomplishing great deeds such as the creation of the universe! In Neterian religion, there is no concept of a devil or daemon, the way we understand them now. Rather, it is understood that the forces of entropy are constantly working in nature to bring that which has been constructed by human hands to their original natural state. The serpent Apep (Apophis), who daily tries to stop Ra's boat of creation, is the symbol of entropy. Entropy increases as matter and energy in the universe degrade to an ultimate state of inert uniformity. Set protects the boat of Ra from the forces of entropy (Apep).

The cosmogonies of Heliopolis, Memphis, Hermopolis and Thebes belong to the Egyptian myth in their quality of themes presenting the first stages of a genesis (that is the three *creative* stages). The role of the creative cause is attributed differently in each theme, according to the stage to which this theme refers. The order of the principles which are active in each stage may vary according to the "product" of that stage; but the way of expressing it depends upon the angle from which it is considered. [56] The theme of Heliopolis is that of the abstract character of the Beginning and Constant Creation. It begins with the creation in principle, out of inert original chaos. In the theme taught at Memphis, the creative Principle is the heavenly fire Ptah, which has descended into the Primordial Earth, which through Ptah surges from the chaos. The theme of Hermopolis

---

[55] Iamblichus, 2006 translation. (p. 304)
[56] Schwaller de Lubicz, I. 1978. (p. 338)

is an entering into operation within concrete Nature. Seen in this light, these elements of a theogony establish a "Hierarchy of the Neters,' similar to those found in other traditions- Hindu, Hebrew, Cabbala, etc.- but unlike these, not "dogmatized"; a hierarchy depending on the order of their appearance as primary or secondary causes, and on the nature of their functions: spiritual, subtile, or material. To express ourselves more clearly, we speak of the "Celestial," "Intermediate" and "Terrestrial" worlds.[57]

Egyptian-Greek Synthesis – the Hermetic Cosmology

"The Mind, O Tat, is of the very Essence of God, if yet there be any Essence of God…. Wherefore we must be bold to say, that an Earthly Man is a Mortal God, and that the heavenly God, is an Immortal Man."

-Hermes Trismegistus-

Comparisons between Pythagorean and Hermetic literature are certainly very instructive. There are many formal similarities, and overlaps in subject matter, between Pythagorean and the Hermetic pseudepigrapha.[58]

Pythagoreans to some extent influenced the flow of magical tradition because they themselves were swimming in the stream- not because they were directing it. Pythagoreanism wrapped itself around other traditions, and other traditions wrapped themselves around it. This looseness and flexibility of Pythagoreanism's relationship to other apparently distinct traditions is especially manifest in the case of its relationship with Hermeticism and Hermetic texts.[59] Pythagorean traditions

---

[57] Schwaller de Lubicz, I. 1978. (p. 305)
[58] Kingsley, P. 1995. (p. 321)
[59] Kingsley, P. 1995. (p. 333)

did find its way into Egypt- and particularly into Graeco-Egyptian magical papyri. On the other hand, in recent years it has become increasingly clear how closely the writings ascribed to Hermes Trismegistus- themselves very much a product of Greek culture in Egypt- are related to these same magical papyri.

Hellenism was politically successful in Egypt, but in cultural terms, Egypt, with its ancient traditions of more than two thousand years, remained Egyptian. Because Egyptian culture was so progressive and cosmopolitan, the Greeks were eager to discover Egypt's ancient wisdom. As any foreign culture would, they translated, and then interpreted those traditions and beliefs into their own way of thinking. From this blending of Egyptian and Greek scholarship arose the mythical figure Hermes Trismegistus. Hermes Trismegistus was distinctly human and hellenized.

The essence of this figure was a unification of the Greek Hermes and the Egyptian Thoth- Thoth being the Greek translation for the Egyptian god Djeheuty. The Greek Hermes, known for his wisdom, was the son of Zeus and the messenger of the gods. Thoth was principle of transformation, or death and rebirth. His role was so great in Egyptian thought that he was deemed responsible for cosmic order, as well as society's institutions. As such, he was "the measurer" and the "measurer of time." Thoth presided over Temple cults, the calendar, and legislation, as well as sacred rituals, the composition of texts, and the science and magic of the arts related to alchemy. However, it was in his role in the afterlife as a guide to the departed and the judgment of the dead that Thoth was most famous. [60]

Consequently, newcomers to Egypt identified with Thoth through a native likeness from their home culture.[61] With the Greeks, Hermes revealed the divine- the Logos. Egypt's tradition of Thoth grew into the belief that he had written forty-two books, which contained knowledge humankind needed. This in

---

[60] Fowden, G. 1997.
[61] Malkowski, E.F. 2007. (p. 285)

turn grew into the literature we know today as the teachings of Hermes Trismegistus, also Thoth the Thrice Great. [62]

The Corpus Hermeticum is a collection of essays devoted to philosophically describing humankind, nature, the cosmos, and deity. Written in a dialogue style, the essays focus on the cosmogonic and cosmological and are distinctly a strong interpretation of the anthropic principle. At the core of these texts is the role of man and man's relationship to nature and cosmos. The immediate, observable world is explained as a manifestation of the abstract mind that can be comprehended only by understanding the nature of one's Self.

In the first essay, Hermes receives a vision explaining creation. In his vision, everything becomes light, and within the light darkness forms that is described as a coiling phenomenon, in "sinuous folds" like a snake. Representing matter (earth), this "coiling" soon transforms into water. Then through Logos (Word), active light (fire) appears from within the water. According to the text, the Light is the "Mind of God," and the Logos "the Son of God."[63]

God is not so much a person in the Hermetic view as a conceptual understanding of what nature is. Only silence can express God's true name. God is self-cause and self-sufficiency. The essence of God is Mind. From Mind comes forth Logos, representing the principles that constitute everything that exists. Also within Mind is the "Archetypal Form," which becomes the details of the physical reality, which exists prior to the creation of matter. Energies are part of God, regardless of whether they are matter, body, or essence.

From Logos the abstract cosmos is born, and from the abstract cosmos, the physical cosmos is created, meaning that Mind (God) created, in God's image, another second Mind that is the abstract cosmos. This second Mind is also referred to as the

---

[62] Malkowski, E.F. 2007. (p. 287)
[63] Corpus Hermeticum. (p. 1)

"Formative Mind." If space is God's creation, then it is substance. However, if it is God Himself, it transcends substance.

To explain why consciousness exists, it is said that matter shares in Mind (abstract cosmos) as an equal to the Mind of God. In other words, God became form in the existence of the cosmos and became the archetypal Man. Thus, the following anthropic principle is declared: "Man's true nature is abstract, and the physical cosmos is a result of that nature."

Within Man there is also a mind, so he also has the ability to conceptualize the bodiless, self-existing Mind. Yet, many men are unaware of this, because Darkness (unknowing) is the basis of material form that was fashioned through water. For mankind, God is intelligible, meaning humans can conceptualize and contemplate God's existence. Thought always occurs beneath the thinker's essence. So, being below God's essence, man can think of God. On the other hand, since there can be nothing above God, then God can never think of Himself. Therefore, God thinks of Himself as being nothing else but what He thinks.

Mind, because of reason, is the principle of Man. Reason lies in the soul, which lies in the spirit, which lies in the body. Mind and Reason are also Man's Archetypal Soul. Without Mind, men reason in a fashion similar to that of animals, with their feelings and impulses. Without Mind, Man is concerned only with bodily pleasures, believing that this is the nature of being. By not identifying with the material world, the nature of the Self becomes apparent. With the identification and recognition of the Self as an unknown abstract entity, the source (Mind) becomes the true understanding or reality. Achieving this understanding is gnosis. Not only does gnosis show piety to God, but it also defines Man as God. In "the Key," essay ten, God's energy is described as God's will and through the contemplation of self-causality and self-existing (Greek "good"), the goal of man is that his soul should become like God. [64]

The dispensation of all things are derived not by the means of Two (Cosmos and Man), but through the One. God contains the cosmos and the cosmos contains Man. The cosmos therefore, is God's Son- Man, as it was- the Cosmos's Child. The dispensation of the universe is through the nature of the One who pervades all things through the Mind. Without Mind, the soul can neither speak nor act.

Because it is impossible to conceptualize nothing, think of yourself as deathless and able to know all arts, all sciences, and all ways of life. Become higher than any height and lower than any depth, then collect into yourself the senses of all creatures and all the elements. The Hermeticist asks, "Is God Unseen?" and answers, "Who is more manifest than God?" Nothing is unseen, even things without a body. Mind sees itself in thinking, God in making.

If we compare some of the earlier Pythagorean writings, and that of the Hermetica, it becomes clear that what was considered important by the authors in both cases was an inner sense of revelation capable of pointing to the real nature and significance of the things outwardly observed. [65]

---

[64] Corpus Hermeticum. (p. 32)
[65] Kingsley, P. 1995. (p. 373)

"On the other hand the Pythagoreans, because they see many qualities of numbers in bodies perceived by sense, regard objects as numbers, not as separate numbers, but as derived from numbers. And why? Because the qualities of numbers exist in harmony both in the heaven and in many other things. But for those who hold that number is mathematical only, it is impossible on the basis of their hypothesis to say any such thing; and it has already been remarked that there can be no science of these numbers. However, we say, as above, that there is a science of numbers. Evidently, the mathematical does not exist apart by itself, for in that case its qualities could not exist in bodies. In such a matter the Pythagoreans are restrained by nothing ; when, however, they construct out of numbers physical bodies out of numbers that have neither weight nor lightness, bodies that have weight and lightness - they seem to be speaking about another heaven and other bodies than those perceived by sense."

-Aristotle-

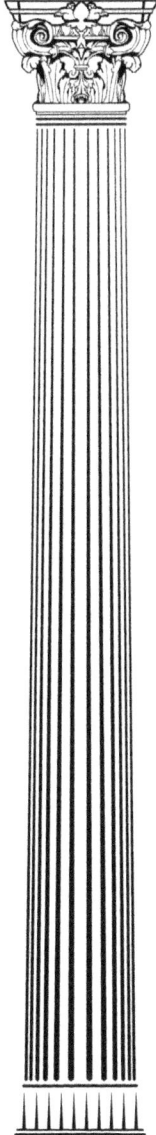

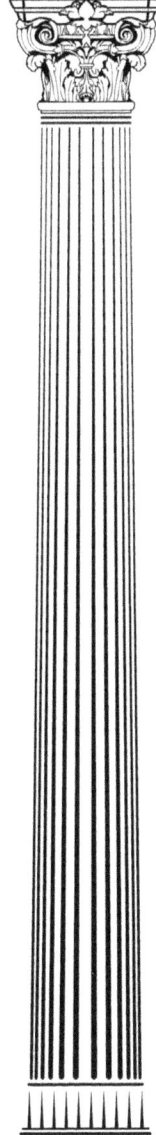

PART II

THEORY

INTRODUCTION

*"Science enables us to take advantage of the continuity of
Nature by the empirical application of certain principles whose
interplay involves different orders of idea connected with each
other in a way beyond our present comprehension."*

-Aleister Crowley-

As Initiates in the Left-Hand Path, our primary aim is to Self-create by introducing change. We choose a path that provides the most appropriate tools and apply them to create order from this chaos introduced by the change. The tools we choose should resonate with the individual Self and provide results that support the individual quest towards immortality. There has to be a basic structure that defines the route we take, otherwise it becomes undirected and senseless and we become victim to the material daemons that haunt this world.

It is impossible to achieve immortality unless we conceptualize the world in which we want to be it. If you want to bring about change within your universe, you need to have an understanding of how it is made up. This understanding, otherwise defined as a cosmology, provides a mechanism through which we bring about real change. Without it, we can achieve nothing.

The Left-Hand Path is one of freedom, in which we have the choice to develop our own understanding of the universe. Yet, it is unfortunate that many Magicians confuse this freedom of choice with not having a personal cosmology as a primary requirement for achieving success in the practice of Magic. Then, when we choose a Magical System, we get so involved in the practice of its Magic, that we become unaware that the method is, in fact, based on someone else's understanding of the universe! It is only then, much later on, when we have made some basic progress that we reach a point where the System just does not work as good as it did in the beginning. We then fall into a trap realizing the complexities of most cosmologies, blaming the System that it does not work.

It is therefore, important that we first investigate and understand the basic premises, or cosmology, on which each System is based, before we endeavor in its practice. It is only then that we can properly make use of its advanced applications. In addition, as responsible Magicians we need to ascertain whether the basic premises of any System is compatible with that of our own. This is a basic requirement for those that want to personalize their magic. After all, the Left-Hand Path is one of individuality and not of the blind following of any rules or dogma.

Developing a personal cosmology is a difficult task, especially for the uninitiated. Science failed to provide a proper cosmology with its rhetoric, since it cannot coherently explain the origin of that which lies beneath the concrete; and religion failed in its dogma, since it cannot coherently explain the origin of the universe. For the most part, we are therefore, left in the dark.

The Pythagorean Number System is a valuable tool for those Initiates that want to develop an individualized cosmology. The System forces one towards resolving important issues, such as those related to the origin/ source and qualities of the cosmos, and the positioning of the Self in relation to the gods/god/neters/archetypes/angels/daemons that are manifest in your universe, whether you approach them theistically, or non-theistically. It provides structure to your understanding of the world you live in, based on a system of logic.

Once the individual has developed an understanding of his or her own cosmology, it is also possible to re-apply these principles back into the System, and create through them a structured and individualized approach towards Initiation. The Ceremony of the Nine Angles is an excellent example of such. In the same way it serves as an approach towards understanding the universe, it also serves as a valid and reliable approach towards understanding the universe inside ourselves. In this capacity, it serves as an invaluable tool for Black Magic. Only few Systems provide this level of flexibility.

The Pythagorean Number System dates back centuries. In fact, it is so old that contemporary occult science and philosophy is in disrepute over its exact origin. Yet, what we do know is that magicians, philosophers and even societies as a whole, at some stage, have successfully applied the System as a way of life, and that those who did, stood out as the most influential of their time. The Pythagorean Number System therefore, is much more than just a method of practice we reserve for the magical chamber. The System becomes the foundation of a focused lifestyle, directed according to the individual Desires, and manifest by the Will of the practicing Black Magician. Its flexibility allows for a very broad audience, even so outside the realm of Magic. The advantage in this is that when a Magical System also becomes the tool used for steering the mundane, life as a whole becomes magical! Indeed, this is what the Pythagorean Number System does. This is as close as we can Become in the like of our gods.

Within the realm of magic, the Pythagorean Number System can be applied as a method of, but is not limited to, Theurgy. Theurgy, as will be explained, serves as an appropriate vehicle for any Left-Hand Path initiate, to travel the path of Self-discovery and eventual Self-deification. Traces of the practice of Theurgy have been left behind in the work of some of the most influential thinkers of both antiquity and our time, more so than can be said of any other system of magic. It is therefore, important that we, in the second part of this chapter, also have a closer look at Theurgy and those fundamental principles it is based on. It is envisaged that this section should provide the reader with a sufficient understanding of the principles of both the Pythagorean Number System and Theurgy, and that this could, eventually, be used to develop an individualized method of practice.

"Mathematics might be prized or ignored, but it is equally true everywhere- independent of ethnicity, culture, language, religion, ideology"

-Carl Sagan, The Demon-Hunted World-

In nature, number is function and any calculative approach to number, whatever the approach may be, ceases to be a function and becomes a description. Although number is abstract, it is usually associated with a quantity, or physical objects or at least the description of a physical aspect. In rationalistic, calculative thinking, number is the halting of activity and finality. It is therefore, passive. It provides a way to compare and perceive. In functional thinking, number is active, just as nature. Everything in nature is in constant motion. The nature of activity is function, which leads to consequence. The activity of subatomic particles results in atoms. The activity of atoms results in elements. The activity of elements results in compounds, which leads to celestial bodies.

Any function has a force, a method and an outcome.[66] The outcome, which is the result of the function, will vary depending on the method of the function. This method is what leads to diversity. This variation in method is what we understand as quantity, which is what we label as number. Thus, number creates nature.

With regard to the esoteric character of number, we must avoid the following mistake: Two is not One plus One; it is not a composite, it is the multiplying power; it is the consciousness of multiplication; it is the multiplying Work; it is the notion of the plus in relation to the minus; it is a new unity; it is sexuality; it is the origin of Nature; physis, the neter Two. As we progress from

---

[66] Malkowski, E.F. 2007. (p. 97)

one number to another, each number not only symbolizes and defines the specific function allotted to it, but incorporates all combinations of functions leading to it.

One, the Monad

"In the beginning was the Word [Logos], and the Word was with God, and the Word was God. He was in the beginning with God; all things were made through Him, and without Him nothing was made that was made."

-John 1:1-3-

The absolute state is the first number: the irreducible One. All manifestation is therefore initially a result of addition, and then of multiplication of this first Unity. It builds the foundation for understanding the abstract. It is the non-spatial source of Number. [67] It is called "monad" because of its stability, since it preserves the specific identity of any number with which it is conjoined (2 x 1 = 2; 3 x 1 = 3). The monad organized everything, because it contains everything potentially (even if they are not yet actual). The monad holds seminally the principle contained within all subsequent numbers. Nicomachus said that God coincides with the Monad, since he is seminally everything that exists. As the result of this conception of the "Supreme," when

---

[67] Waterfield, R. 1988. (p. 35)

it ventures not only to denominate it, through ineffable, but also to assert something of its relation to other things, it considers this as preeminently its peculiarity, that it is *the principle of principles.*"[68] It is necessary from these premises, since there is only one Monad, as the principle of the universe, that this unity should produce from itself, prior to everything else, a multitude of natures (being, life, intellect, soul, nature, and body) and these natures are no other than the Gods!

The monad, however, is also intelligence, for intelligence sees according to the Monad. As for example, men are made up of many parts, and part by part, they are devoid of sense, comprehension, and experience. Yet, we perceive that man as one alone, whom no being resembles, possesses these qualities; and we perceive that a horse is one, but part by part, it is without experience.

The Monad produces itself and is produced from itself, since it is self-sufficient and has no power set over it, and is everlasting; and it is evidently the cause of permanence. Therefore, they say that the Monad is not only God, but also intellect, since it is not yet manifesting anything actual, but everything is conceptually together in it. [69] In short, they consider it to be the seed of all, and both male and female at once.

> "Whether the one itself is a sort of essence, as first the Pythagoreans and later Plato, affirmed."
>
> -Aristotle-

Likewise, they call it "Chaos," which is Hesiod's first generator, because Chaos gives rise to everything else, as the Monad does.

---

[68] Taylor, T. 2006. (p. x)
[69] Waterfield, R. 1988. (p. 39)

Other names: mixture, blending, obscurity, darkness, thanks to the lack of articulation and distinction of everything that ensues from it; cause of truth, simple, paradigm, life and Proteus.

Two, the Dyad

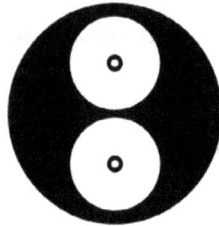

Two expresses fundamental opposition, polarization. Polarity is fundamental to all phenomena: Set – Horus, plus – minus, day – night, man – women, logic – reason. Heraclitus believed that all opposites (qualities) are simultaneously present in nature, and that harmony, which makes physical reality what it is, consists of opposing tension. It is important to realize that in a perfectly dual system there can exist no form of discrimination between the opposing forces. In fact, the one cannot exist without the other. It therefore contains the principle of equality. It is divisible into both equal and unequal parts, but the Dyad alone cannot be divided into unequal parts; and also, when it is divided into equal parts, is completely unclear to which class its parts belong, as it is like a source. The Pythagoreans called the Dyad opinion, because truth and falsity lie in opinion; movement, generation, change, division, length, multiplication, addition, kinship, and relativity.[70] The undefined dyad is science; fittingly, for all proof and all persuasion is part of science, and farther every syllogism brings together what is questioned out of some things that are agreed upon, and easily proves

[70] Waterfield, R. 1988. (p. 41)

something else; and science is the comprehension of these things, wherefore it would be the dyad.

Apart from recklessness, they think that, because it is the very first to have endured separation, it deserves to be called anguish, endurance and hardship.

The Dyad remains without form and without the limitation of being contained by three terms and proportionality, and as it were, the source and foundation of the diversity of numbers. The Dyad gets its name from passing through asunder, for the Dyad is the first to have separated itself from the Monad.

Other names: Isis, justice, Nature (since its movement towards being), Diometor (the mother of Zeus), Rhea. Its ruling planet is the moon.

Three, the Triad

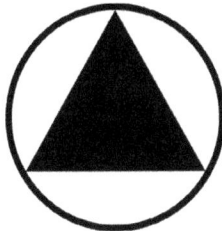

"For as the Pythagoreans say, the all and all things are defined by threes; for end and middle and beginning constitute the number of the all, and also the number of the triad."

-Aristotle-

Three- the Force that holds Two apart (or keeps it apart)! The heart, not head, understands Three. We cannot know it by the rational faculties; we understand it- love desire, affinity, attraction, repulsion, interaction. It is also the Number of the Holy Trinity. It is the number of Thoth, the Three times Great!

One of the early Greek philosophers, Heraclitus (535-475 BCE), believed that the world is composed of a unity of opposites and that these opposites succeed each other. Only a single property is exposed at a time. Heraclitus used the example of a bow: when the bowstring is pulled one way (by one end of the bow) and the other way (by the other end), the tension between these opposing forces allows the bow to perform its function. So beneath the apparently motionless exterior of the bowstring is the constant tension between opposed forces. In the system, a coherent, unified, and stable composite is produced. In taking this to the extreme, if the balance between opposites were not maintained, then the tension (unity) would also cease to exist. Three represents this balance.

According to Pythagorean cosmogony, Three is the magic number for identifying the nature of deity as it relates to creation. Aristotle made the following comment:

"For, as the Pythagoreans say, the world and all that is in it is determined by the number three, since the beginning and middle and end give the number of an "all" and the number they give is the triad. And so, having taken these three from nature as (so to speak) laws of it, we make further use of the number three in the worship of the Gods." [71]

This concept of the Divine being composed of three terms provided the basis for the Triangle as the most profound of all geometrical symbols. For the Greeks the letter *D* (Delta, or Δ) became "the vehicle of the Unknown Deity." [72]

---

[71] Aristotle, De Caelo, 398.

[72] The Pythagorean Science of Numbers. **Theosophy,** 27(7): 301-306, May 1939.

The idea of relating Christ to the Unknown God of Greece would later have great theological ramifications, giving birth to the Trinitarian concept. What is interesting about this is that it is believed that the trinity was not the invention of the Christian movement itself, but a synthesis of existing Pythagorean beliefs into a new framework. [73]

The Triad is the very first to make actual the potentialities of the Monad- oddness, perfection, proportionality, unification, limit. [74] Three is unique, as it is the only number to be equal to the sum of all preceding numbers (1 + 2 = 3). They call it mean and proportion. We invoke the dead three times. They call the Triad "piety": hence, the name "Triad" is derived from "terror," that is, fear and caution. [75]

Anatolius said that the Triad, the first odd number, is called perfect by some, because it is the first number to signify the totality- beginning, middle and end. Nicomachus said that Three is the source in actuality of number, which is by definition a system of Monads. The Triad is the first to be a system, of Monad and Dyad. The Triad is the form of the completion of all things.

---

[73] Malkowski, E.F. 2007. (p. 178)
[74] Waterfield, R. 1988. (p. 49)
[75] Waterfield, R. 1988. (p. 51)

Four, the Tetrad

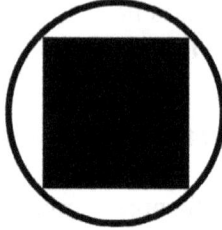

Everything in the universe turns out to be completed in the natural progression up to the Tetrad. Material, substance, things; the physical world is the matrix of all sensuous experiences. Two and Three do not account for substance. Man, women and love does not implicate marriage. Four represents the basic elements of matter- earth, water, fire and air (wind). It is the *principle of substantiality.* It represents the cross on which Christ, the cosmic man, is crucified. By reconciling its polarities through his own consciousness, he attains unity.

The Tetrad provides the limit of corporeality and three-dimensionality. [76] The pyramid, which is the minimal solid and the one, which first appears, is obviously contained within a tetrad. Four are the foundations of wisdom- arithmetic, music, geometry, and astronomy- ordered 1, 2, 3 and 4. Because the tetrad is like this, people used to swear by Pythagoras because of it. There are four sources of the universe- the Monad, matter, form and result. There are four elements and their powers. There are four traditional seasons of the year, four distinct senses in living creatures (for touch is a common background to the other four), and four kinds of virtues.

Anatolius called the Tetrad "justice," since the square, which is based on it, is equal to the perimeter.

---

[76] Waterfield, R. 1988. (p. 55)

Five, the Pentad

To describe the knowable Universe, three dimensions are required, and time (perception of movement) as well as quality as it relates to quantity (the specific and intrinsic characteristics of an object). So five factors are naturally involved in describing the universe, as well as the absolute state (infinity) in which it exists.[77] Five is the first "universal" number, the number of "life." It is quality fully quantified. From the roots of Two, Three and Five all the harmonic proportions can be derived. It provides the key to the vitality of the universe, its creative nature. Five contains 1, 2, 3, and 4, the sum of which is 10, and thereby the archetypal universe is created. The absolute state, in its manifestation as the concrete world represented by numbers, takes form when it reaches 10. It is therefore also the number of potentiality, which exists outside time. The five-point star also represents the idea of to "become one of the company of Ra."

Schwaller de Lubicz declares that the impulse to all form and to all movement is given by Φ.... Phi is the impulse for the whole number 5, but ... Φ cannot be defined in rational numbers. It can only be defined through the harmony that it engenders.[78]

The Pentad is the first number to encompass the specific identity of all number, since it encompasses 2, the first even

---

[77] Malkowski, E.F. 2007. (p. 111)
[78] Schwaller de Lubicz, R.A. 1998. (Volume II)

number, and 3, the first odd number. Hence, it is called "marriage," since it is formed of male and female. [79] The Pentad is particularly comprehensive of the natural phenomena of the universe. They called the Pentad "lack of strife," not only because aether, the fifth element, which is set apart on its own, remains unchanging, while there is strife and change among the things under it. The Pentad is also highly expressive of justice, and justice comprehends all the other virtues. The Pentad has neither excess nor defectiveness in it, and it will turn out to provide this property to the rest of the numbers that follow it.

Other names: They call the Pentad Nemesis. It distributes the heavenly, divine, and physical elements by means of five. Because it levels out inequality, they call it "Providence." It is also "Bubastian," because of being honored at Bubastos in Egypt; "Aphrodite," because it binds to each other a male and female number. Likewise, it is called "nuptial," "androgyny," and "demigod," because in its special diagram it is assigned the central place. It is called "immortal" and "Pallas," because it reveals the fifth essence.

Six, the Hexad

The hexad is the first perfect number.[80] The actualization of potentiality, within the framework of time and space. It is

---

[79] Waterfield, R. 1988. (p. 66)
[80] Waterfield, R. 1988. (p. 75)

therefore called the "Number of the material world." Numbers 1 to 5 are invisible. Six is different. Volume requires six directions. Six is also represented by the cube, often used as a throne by the Pharaoh, used as a symbol of actualization in space. It is called "marriage," as it arises not from addition like Pentad, but by multiplication.

If the soul gives articulation and composition to the body, just as soul at large does to formless matter, and if no number whatsoever can be more suited to the soul than the Hexad, then no other number could be said to be the articulation of the universe, since the Hexad is found stably to be the maker of soul and causer of the condition of life (hence the word "hexad").

The Pythagoreans, following Orpheus, called the Hexad "wholeness of limbs," because the whole- that is the universe- has been divided into parts and is harmonious thanks to it.

Other names: The Hexad is called reconciliation, peace, health, anvil, hurler of missiles, preside over crossroads, Amphitrite (because it yields two perfect triangles), dweller of justice (because of its placing next to the Pentad), Thaleia (because of its harmonizing different things), and panacea.

Seven, the Heptad

Six terms are insufficient to account for the process of "coming-into-being." It is the number of growth. Seven is the seed that, through formative growth, becomes the manifest object. Seven terms (factors) constitute the cosmos in appearance.[81] Seshat, which means seven, is the female counterpart of Thoth, therefore mistress of measure. Seven terms are needed to account for the principle of growth. Phenomena tend to complete in seven stages. Many things, both in the heavens of the universe and on the Earth, are in fact, brought to completion by Seven. That is why it is called "Chance," because it accompanies everything which happens, and "critical time," because it has gained the most critical position and nature. There are seven tones in the harmonic scale. Libra, the Balance, is the seventh sign.

Seven is not born of any mother and is a virgin. It is the number of the primary concord, the fourth 4:3, and of geometric proportion (1, 2, 4). It is called "that which brings to completion."[82] Seven is critical in illnesses. We perceive seven things- body, distance, shape, size, color, movement and rest. There are seven movements.

Nicomachus of Gerasa called the Heptad "forager," because its structure has been collected and gathered together in a manner resembling unity. Moreover, it is called "guardian'" for there are seven that guard the universe and keep it in continuous and eternal stability.

Other names: "Athena" (because it is a virgin and unwed).

---

[81] Schwaller De Lubicz, R.A. 1981.
[82] Waterfield, R. 1988. (p. 87)

Eight, the Ogdoad

The eighth zodiac, Scorpio, traditionally symbolizes death, sex, renewal. It is a renewal of self-replication. In Egypt, the text declares: "I am One, who becomes Two, who Becomes Four, who Becomes Eight, and then I am One again." It corresponds to the physical world as we experience it. It represents the first actual cube. All the ways in which it is put together are excellent and equilibrated tunings. The Ogdoad is called "the embracer of all harmonies." So, when they call it "Cadmean," they should be understood to be referring to the fact that, as all historians tell us, Harmonia was the wife of Cadmus. The number eight is the source of the musical ratios.

The Pythagoreans used to call the Ogdoad "mother," since Rea is the mother of the gods and the Ogdoad an extension of Rhea. With the Ogdoad, things come by love, friendship, wisdom and creative thought.[83]

Anatolius calls the Ogdoad "safety" and "foundation," since it is a leader, because Two is a leader: the seed of the Ogdoad is the first even number. The eighth sphere encompasses the whole- hence the saying "All is eight."[84]

---

[83] Waterfield, R. 1988. (p. 103)
[84] Waterfield, R. 1988. (p. 103)

Nine, the Ennead

Ancient and modern traditions are replete with nine-fold symbolism. The Norse God Odin, ruler of the 9 Norse worlds, hung 9 days on the world axis or Yggdrasil tree to win the secrets of wisdom for humankind. In Scandinavia, 9-day fertility feasts were held every 9 years. There were nine Norse giantesses, who strode 9 paces at a time and lived at the edge of the sea and land. The city of Troy in Homer's Iliad and Oddessey was besieged for 9 years, while Odysseus wandered for 9 more years in trying to return home. The Greek goddess, Demeter, was depicted with nine ears of wheat and searched 9 days for her daughter Persephone. The birth of Apollo and Artemis by Leto took 9 days and nights (Artemis becoming the midwife in the process and later choosing two 9-year old girls as her companions). The Greeks also honored nine *muses*, while the Egyptians honored a company of nine "gods" or *neteru*. Egyptian pharaohs, meanwhile, were often symbolized by 9 bows. Celtic traditions talk of nine Celtic maidens and 9 virgins attending Bridget, while the sacred Beltane fire rites were attended by a cycle of 9 groups of 9 men. Aztec, Mayan, and Native American myths describe nine cosmic levels (four above, earth, and four below). As the most auspicious number of celestial power in ancient Chinese, nine became the rule in nine great social laws, 9 classes of officials, 9 sacred rites, and 9-story pagodas. The festival of the "double *yang*" was held on the 9th hour of the 9th day of the 9th month. In Christian symbolism, there are nine orders of angelic choirs in nine circles of heaven and nine orders of devils within nine rings of hell -- possibly accounting for the fact that it took 9 days for Lucifer and his angels to fall from heaven.

The ennead is the greatest of the numbers and is an unsurpassable limit.[85] It is complex and almost insusceptible of expression. Nine represents the Great Ennead-interpenetrating, interacting, and interlocked. It emanates from the Absolute, or "Central Fire." It is the symbolic analog of the original Unity. It is an expression of metaphysical reality. In numerical relationships it represents the basics of harmony. Where seven terms constitute the cosmos in appearance, nine terms constitute it as fact.

In pi, Schwaller de Lubicz finds that the relation of the circle's diameter to its circumference is the same as the relation of 1 to 9. In his own words, pi is the equivalent of saying "Nothing exists without the life of the Spirit."

The ennead marks the end of the formation of specific entities. There is natural progression up to it, but after it, there is repetition. Other evidence led them to call it "Prometheus," because it prevents any number from proceeding further than itself. [86]

Other names: The Ennead is called "concord" and "limitation," and also "sun," in the sense that it gathers things together. It is called "lack of strife," "assimilation" (because it is the first odd square), "Hephaestus" (because the way up to it is, as it were, by smelting and evaporation), "Hera" (because the sphere of air falls under it), "sister-consort of Zeus" (because of its being paired with the monad), "banisher" (because it prevents the voluntary progress of number), and finishing point.

---

[85] Waterfield, R. 1988. (p. 105)
[86] Waterfield, R. 1988. (p. 106)

From the Abstract to the Concrete

"In an old Sanskrit book there is a verse which describes the essential elements of a picture. The first in order is *Vrúpa-bhédáh*--"separateness of forms." Forms are many, forms are different, each of them having its limits. But if this were absolute, if all forms remained obstinately separate, then there would be a fearful loneliness of multitude. But the varied forms, in their very separateness, must carry something which indicates the paradox of their ultimate unity, otherwise there would be no creation."

-Rabindranath Tagore-

Pythagoreans regard numbers as the philosophical basis of cosmic genesis. When we investigate the nature of number- its existence in relation to consciousness and perception- we deal with alchemical and/or Hermetic aspects- while its revelation that has to do with measure, we may call the Pythagorean aspect. In this sense, Hermetic and Pythagorean aspects are two aspects of a single coin- like the Monad, from which emanates the world, and then the matter that represents this world. Measure is the means by which matter becomes manifest as form. Such matter, generally speaking, is "potential" and exists as "substance" before all worlds and manifested states, waiting only to be cognized into existence. Matter is what is measured, measure in this sense a determination of potentiality. Measure is thus intimately related, on the one hand, to number, on the other hand, to order or harmony. Measure, then, mediates order, which is a vision or illumination- "Let there be Light."

The "abstract of numbers," means the *vital bond* that exists between things. The "concrete nature of numbers," means the *manifestation of life* under its many material, accidental aspects: weight, density, color, etc.[87] These two aspects of

---

[87] Schwaller de Lubicz, R.A. 1986. (p. 30)

number have a common function: succession, by which the past, the present, and simultaneity, as well as the future, are defined. Everything may therefore, be traced back to numbers, which are the last (or first) manifestation of matter, and the first cause of the creative idea, which is the energetic image of the form that it generates. Numbers constitute the principle of life, the vital impulse of cosmos. To understand true succession in creation, one must know how the first, or abstract, nature of numbers develops- how multiplicity disengages itself from Unity.

In the geometric unfolding of numbers, each dimension functions as the principle and limit of the dimension that it contains and of which it is the boundary. The "point" is the limit of the "line," the "line" is the limit of the "plane," and the "plane" is the limit of the "volume." In each stage the limit is "outside" and therefore "contained" what it limits. [88] In order for a volume to become manifest, it must be limited by a plane; the plane, in turn, must be limited by a line; and the line, in turn, must be limited by a point. It is important to acknowledge here that according to Iamblichus a line should not be conceived as a "collection of many points" and, strictly speaking, has no dimension at all. The transition from point to line occurs only when a fundamental change takes place in the orientation of the point, to be precise: when it begins to *flow*. The line is the flow of the point. From this, we deduct the following:

1) The point is the principle of expression;
2) The point realizes its limiting power in the manifestation of the line;
3) The line realizes its limiting power in the manifestation of the plane;
4) The plane realizes its limiting power in the manifestation of the volume.

---

[88] Shaw, G. 1951. (p. 213)

It is clear that one may speak of genesis if- when a dimension is extended to pass into another- the original dimension produces its effect by *imposing a form*, by serving as a limit.

Everything that exists within this cosmos has only two characteristics- i) quantity and ii) quality. Quantity is easy to understand since it is the most obvious concept we experience. Quantity therefore, is objective. Not only can we see quantity, but we can also feel it. It is fixed. Quality, on the other hand, is subjective and not so easy to understand. Quality is abstract and subject to change. One cannot explain quality; one can only merge oneself with it and thus feel it. What Schwaller de Lubicz expressed in his philosophy is that quality exists in a non-dimensional state and that quality represents the essence of the core of our Being. Numbers are the purest expression of the truth because they determine the exact relation between cause and effect. Numbers can be used to specify the dates (duration, time, year, lunar month, etc.) of cosmic genesis, both on a macrocosmic and microcosmic level. From Numbers, the magician will know all the essential conditions necessary for the development (birth, life and "death") of all things.[89]

Every cosmic phenomenon comes to realization in three stages- i) polarization, ii) ideation and iii) formation. The first stage of polarization is characterized by "generic selection," that is the causal circle. It is obvious that the first Unity, the cause without a cause, is indivisible. It is the first Unity, or Monad. It is purely qualitative, without quantity. Yet, it serves as a reference of quantity. The first *"Irreducible One"* can only create multiplicity by qualitative addition, and never by multiplication (1 times 1 is 1; 1 plus 1 is 2). It therefore, is the point that generates lines by addition, since it cannot manifest itself in any other way. It is in this way, then, that 1 gives 1 and 1, or

---

[89] Schwaller de Lubicz, R.A. 1986. (p. 35)

I

I   I

and is by this fact, Three. This number, in its abstract nature, is Two.

In the cycle of Ideation, the first polarity- that has necessarily become the new cause- is distinguished by "energetic creation." It is not yet manifest as number Two. This means that in order to constitute the root of its future from, the first pole establishes lines of force whose quantity and quality vary with its nature. It is a complement thereof.

Polarization (stage 1) therefore, is the scission or the cessation of the reason for the existence of a state (i.e. One becomes Two). When the first pole is established, it realizes its own equilibrium by putting itself in energetic communication with other points of "resistance."

Then the marvelous work of organizing and neutralizing the different poles begin. When the generators are selected in the phases of polarization, they arrange themselves in the phase of ideation to fix the energetic shape, and to establish the "potential" skeleton of the physical form. The phase of ideation in becoming is essentially unstable and creative. Each harmonic moment in the universe possesses by this fact its active cause and its passive cause, which is its complement. The "complementation" of these two poles must therefore, have as its effect a new absolute, relative state, the new cause of the new effect. As a result, a cause (whose structure will be fixed in the cycle of formation) or idea (a polar complex having become a unity) associates with other like unities in order to fix the form in three directions- height, depth, and size. Hence, the characteristic of the stage is formative growth.

If life were not dualistic, if there was no Two, there would be no process of multiplication. In addition, it is possible to recognize through Two the dual nature of the Absolute. Two is the manifest nature of the Absolute (a proton and electron form an atom). Remember, quality is number whereby quantity is the measurement that fixes the quality. In essence, this represents the process of the abstract becoming the concrete.[90] Deductively speaking, it must be the case that the abstract Absolute state, the Monad, or Irreducible One, possesses a dual nature. Yet, these two natures exist only potentially and not yet manifestly. This duality is a prime quality of the cosmos.

[*A progression occurred from an Absolute state to a cosmos containing a multitude of objects. It also can be deduced that the absolute state's dual nature, which is both active (masculine) and passive (feminine), must manifest itself. In this, Schwaller de Lubicz finds pure causality for the act of polarization, a desire to separate. The action of polarization is the fact of a scission. From the moment we observe its double nature, we have already provoked the scission- for the One is recognized, by its double nature, to be Two. We thus add a new Unity to the causal Unity, and this new Unity is Two.*]

Within our existing system, we have three distinct natures: i) the Irreducible One, having both active and passive qualities, ii) the manifest passive (feminine), and iii) the manifest active (masculine) natures. Yet, neither (ii) nor (iii) have become individualized or organized. They are still interdependent- it is not possible for the one to exist without the other. Without these numbers there could be no creation. Indeed, from the moment there is activity, there is opposition to it. The manifestation of the active nature necessarily precedes that of the passive nature. Scwaller De Lubicz relates this to the Bible,

---

[90] Schwaller de Lubicz, R.A. 1986. (p. 47)

in which it is said that God created man and made him a companion from one of his ribs so that he would not be alone.

The first active nature, which emerged from the irreducible One, or was created by it, potentially contains in itself also the passive nature. The latter is part of the activity which manifested either as active or passive nature, is from this moment on *androgynous*. The third number (the second part of the two) is "bisexual." It is important here to remember that the Irreducible One can only multiply by addition!

Hence, this triangle has two passive or feminine natures, two active or masculine natures, plus a nature which cannot be defined other than by the very imperfect term "father-mother." Thus, like the number three, the number five is also a creative entity. But, the number five still only constitutes the different non-manifest natures of the three.[91]

In the first polarized number we are dealing with a created being and not yet with a procreated one. Two must devolve to the point of being independent, that is, to the moment when the feminine and masculine natures become individualized and organized. The created must have procreated and the procreated must likewise have procreated in its turn. When the first three unities (One and Two) are defined and have formed the first two numbers, a new polarization occurs: a scission necessary for the manifestation of the two natures. In this respect, it is necessary that we recognize the active nature as quality, force and energy. The passive nature is opposition to activity. Creation will not be concluded until all these natures, existing in a potential state, are manifested one to one- that is, until, they have taken on form, hence quantity. A new polarization occurs- a scission necessary for the manifestation of the two natures. The "new" triangle will therefore be

---

[91] Schwaller de Lubicz, R.A. 1986. (p. 48)

```
         I

       I   I

     I   I   I
```

in which the first two numbers are creators, and are called a "Creative Unity." In this second triangle, we see six natures of the III manifested to the six unities. With the five potential natures of the first triangle, these produce a complex of eleven new and creative "principal natures." Thus, 1, 3, 5 and 11 are bound together, these being the creative numbers, which, indicative of a creative and procreative disequilibrium, we find constantly in nature. The Number III is a harmony in itself. In Three we find three creative possibilities (activity, passivity and product in one). It is therefore, Unity perfectly manifested.

We had the creation of Two by One, the first procreation of Three by Two, and now in Four,

```
         I

       I   I

     I   I   I

   I   I   I   I
```

we shall have procreation by what has been procreated by Three. The IIII contains 4 times 2, plus 1 times the triple nature of the first Triangle, from which we derive the potential manifestation of eleven natures of IIII. This quaternary structure is the last. All natures manifests from it. It is thought of as the most fundamental source of creation- the Creative Spirit or the active principle- that fecundates and maintains the cosmos and all life. Since it has in itself the creative power (11), it can procreate. As Number it is 10, containing and surrounded by the nine principles: the irreducible One, the eternal fecundator. This is the "ineffable, incommunicable Word" of the Kabbalists. It is the creative spirit, the active principle that fecundates and maintains life. It includes the first cause, without a cause.

The Number III is the first complete solution of the creative functions, and, since it is engendered by the first multiplication of II, gives the first procreative state. That is why the Tetragrammaton, and indeed all that archaic or magical symbolism expressed by the number 4, signifies both the last term of creation and the first term of the manifested existence of Being. Creation is to be distinguished from procreation by the fact that it produces by an interior, hence purely qualitative disequilibrium, a quantity that is the formative receptacle of the activity. Procreation, on the other hand, requires an activity working on an independent resistance of the same evolution. The point can only create by addition (division), and the resulting line can only procreate- and never create. A line added to itself, remains a line, whereas as soon as it is multiplied by itself, a line becomes a face. Procreation therefore, is the multiplication of any quantity by itself and results from the addition of a positive, odd (masculine) nature to a negative, even (feminine) nature. Procreation begins with the function of a linear movement, followed by two circular movements (remember, the first face is a triangle). The first perfect triangle is Three (Procreated Unity) and the first perfect square is the quaternary, Four (Absolute Unity). The first perfect form, exists by the addition of two triangles. The first square, which is 4, gives the first perfect form- the cube, which is 16. The Triangle alone cannot give rise to form through the procreating function (multiplication), because a triangle times a triangle gives a face, which is 9. Therefore, the first form exists by the addition of two triangles (which gives the square) and the second, by the multiplication of this square.

The numbers 1, 3, 5 and 7 are the creative numbers since they do not contain any procreated form (they are generated by addition, and do not include any multiplication). They generate all figures and forms, and play, with regard to concrete manifestation, the same role that the irreducible One plays with regard to the abstract world. By addition, these creative numbers can produce other prime or uncomposed (1, 3, 5 and 7) numbers by procreation. These numbers 1, 3, 5 and 7 are therefore, the generators of the stage of ideation (which is only present when creation occurs). Addition of the point gives a line. Multiplication of the line creates the face. By multiplication, similarly, the face will give the form.[92] This completes the cycle of formation.

The square is the perfect face. The perfect form, then, will be that which results from the multiplication of the square- the cube. As the preceding cycles suggest, the face, in order to become the cube, will pass through all the stages of polarization and ideation. The square again, becomes the point- the point of departure for the form. The first pole for the creation of the cube is the face.

The cycle of polarization of the solid therefore, begins with the face, which is one-dimensional only because it possesses a spatial tendency in one direction only, then proceeds to the second dimension in order to become the third dimension. The last phase is the cycle of formation in the cycle of formation. It is always important to recall that each of the three cycles is likewise subdivided into three events (activity, inert reaction, and effect), and that only the cause varies and with it the effect as well. The first cause is the point, the second the line, and the third the face. The cycle of polarization is the phase of addition, whereby the non-dimensional becomes the first dimension- the line. By multiplication, the cycle of ideation gives the second dimension, the face, and thus the face gives the solid by multiplication of a first multiple. In the cycle of formation, the internal separation of the fertile seed's two natures occurs in a way that it predominates, constituting growth of the new seed to maturity, in quantity and in form. That is, Three through

---

[92] Schwaller de Lubicz, R.A. 1986. (p. 65)

movement becomes Four. Seven is the seed (what has been referred to as the face) that, through formative growth, becomes the manifest object.

Table 1 Three Cycles of the Physical World[93]

Cycle	Polarization	Ideation	Formation
Event	Creation	1st Procreation	2nd Procreation
Activity	3	5*	7
Inert Reaction	4	6	8
Effect	5	7	9¥

* 1 active and 1 passive, thus 1 androgyne, a new active cause
¥ By scission, this last cycle produces the two distinct natures that will procreate in what follows

In Number, five is quality fully quantified. Before there can be three dimensions there has to be two, and therefore two, one, and before one, a non-dimensional state exists. These dimensions (number) emerge out of the previous dimension. The Universe must be created from the Absolute though polarization that occurs as an abstraction from One. The universe will be abstract (without form), represented by a single infinitely small point. Now, there are two qualities, since the Absolute state differentiates the universe from itself. As a result, there exists Two, the number 2. For the universe to take shape, we recognize quality must differentiate three more times. First, a second point is created from which a line can be drawn, represented by Three, the number 3. Then it must differentiate into a plane (Four, the number 4) and finally into a volume (Five, or the number 5). Since each state is the product of the previous state, it retains the quality of the previous state. The triangle is actually the first form, having an effect only by addition, but it cannot enjoy the procreating qualities of the perfect form. This means that the triangle is the creative or

---

[93] Malkowski, E.F. 2007. (p. 121)

causal form whose ideal form is the cube. Four times the triangle gives the tetrahedron.

So five contains 1, 2, 3, and 4.[94] The act of the abstract becoming concrete is founded on the idea of harmony (unity) and disharmony. Even numbers (feminine), which are equally divisible, are harmonic and receptive. In other words, they are not creative by themselves. Masculine numbers are disharmonic, cannot be equally divided, and are therefore active and creative. They can be divided only by themselves and by 1. Since 1 contains the masculine as well as the feminine nature, it is considered both odd and even. This mutual action and reaction of the masculine and feminine through polarization, ideation and formation, produces the entire universe, the intangible aspects as well as the tangible. The constant action and reaction of these two natures are best represented in the concept of pi (π), a number that is irrational, since it can be defined only by what it is not. In pi, Schwaller de Lubicz finds that the relation of the circle's diameter to its circumference is the same as the relation of 1 to 9. In his own word, pi is the equivalent of saying "Nothing exists without the life of the Spirit."

Schwaller de Lubicz contends that constant creation is the normal, active state of the cosmos developing through polarization, ideation, and formation. All that exists is generally passive relative to the Absolute. In the Absolute's manifestation as a multiplicity of forms, the first activity, or what is generally referred to as the primordial Scission, alone produces these effects. These effects are the physical cosmos.

---

[94] Malkowski, E.F. 2007. (p. 112)

Summary

Whether the end, or the beginning of all things, there was One, the Monad, irreducible in nature. Two resulted from One, by division, thereby creating Two- the number of Duality. Duality is an essential nature of everything that exists. Without Two, nothing can exist. Yet, it is only through Three that a dynamic relationship in which action and reaction occur, can exist between One and Two. Three, or the Triad, represents the essence of that interaction and the source of all understanding. Four is the first generated number (generated by One, Two and Three), creating the principle of physical existence. Five, the Pentad, is the dynamic manifestation of Four into the physical universe- the creation of space. Six, the Hexad, is the creation of all form as we perceive it and relate to it- the consciousness of man. Seven, the Heptad, is man relating to the One and a realization of man's mystical nature. Eight, the Ogdoad, is a renewal, in that man reaches a new unity analogous to the first unity (a spiritual death and resurrection has taken place). Nine, the Ennead, is the spiritual and mental achievement that a new unity allows. From here, we return to One, which then closes the circle of this process of constant creation.

"Unity transcends consciousness. It is above all division.

The Father of thought- the World- is called CHAOS- the dyad. The number Three, the Mother, is called BABALON. This first triad is essentially Unity, in a manner transcending reason. The comprehension of this Trinity is a matter of spiritual experience. All true Gods are attributed to this Trinity.

An immeasurable Abyss divides it from all manifestations of Reason or the lower qualities of man. In the ultimate analysis of Reason, we find all reason identified with this Abyss. Yet this Abyss is the crown of the mind. Purely intellectual faculties obtain here. This Abyss has no number, for in it all is confusion.

Below this Abyss, we find the moral qualities of Man, of which there are six. The highest is symbolized by the Number Four. Its nature is fatherly; Mercy and Authority are the attributes of its dignity.

The number Five is balanced against it. The attributes of Five are Energy and Justice. Four and Five are again combined and harmonized in the Number Six, whose nature is Beauty and Harmony, mortality and immortality.

In the number Seven, the feminine nature is again predominant, but it is the masculine type of female, the Amazon, who is balanced in the number Eight by the feminine type of male.

In the number Nine we reach the last of the purely mental qualities. It identifies Change with Stability."

-Aleister Crowley with Mary Desti and Leila Waddell-

"He [the Magician] may attract to himself any force of the Universe by making himself a fit receptacle for it, establishing a connection with it, and arranging conditions so that its nature compels it to flow toward him."

-Aleister Crowley-

Introduction

In late Neoplatonism, the spiritual Universe is regarded as a series of emanations from the One, or Monad. This trait is significantly Pythagorean in nature. From the One emanated the Divine Mind (Nous) and in turn from the Divine Mind emanated the World-Soul (Psyche). Neoplatonists insisted that the One is transcendent and in the emanations, nothing of the higher was lost or transmitted to the lower, which remained unchanged by the lower emanations. By using certain techniques, it is possible to identify certain qualities of the Monad, bringing us closer to an understanding of what it is we seek to Become in the like of. Although most Neoplatonists were polytheists, they also embraced monism.

Iamblichus placed human souls near the bottom of the psychic hierarchy. What distinguished embodied souls was the separation of their *ouisai* (essence) and *energeiai* (activities), a hypostatic rupture that condemned them to mortality and separated them from the gods. Theurgy was able to bridge this gap by uniting *energeiai* of mortals with the *energeiai* of the gods. [95] Since the body reflected the activity of the soul, it also indicated the kind of soul that animated it. Nothing would distinguish one incorporeal from another apart from its material

---

[95] Shaw, G. 1951. (p. 73)

expression. Iamblichus stratified the following realms: gods, archangels, angels, daemons, heroes, archons (sublunary), archons (material), and human souls. Their appearances accord with their essences, powers, and energies. For such as they are, such also do they appear to those that invoke them, and they exhibit energies and ideas consentaneous to themselves, and proper indications of themselves. [96]

According to this stratification, human souls were imperfect, lowest, and deficient. Human souls do not have the power to do all things, have the nature to incline and turn toward what they generate and govern (material existence). As lowest of divine beings, the human soul had an unstable and mortal vehicle that alienated it from its own divinity. In embodiment, the soul literally became other to itself. [97] The limits of the soul are conceived as the limits of its mortal body. The soul is capable of performing only one activity: the animation of the body as its vehicle and instrument. The other activity, the inspired acts and intuitions that pertain to the soul's essence, do not derive from the soul but from the gods who use the soul as *their* vehicle.

Why Theurgy?

Theurgy conjoins the soul to the several parts of the universe, and to the total divine powers, which pass through it. It leads the soul to, and deposits it in, the Demiurge, and causes it to be independent of all matter, and to be co-united with the eternal reason alone. Furthermore, it peculiarly connects the soul with the self-begotten and self-moved God, and with the all-sustaining, intellectual, and all-adorning powers of the God, and likewise with that power of him which elevates to truth, and with his self-perfect, effective, and other demiurgic powers. The Theurgic soul then becomes perfectly established in the

---

[96] Iamblichus, 2006 translation. (p. 85)
[97] Shaw, G. 1951. (p. 80)

energies and demiurgic intellections of these powers. It inserts the soul in the whole demiurgic God. [98]

Theurgy versus contemplation

Plotinus urged mental contemplations for those who wished to reunite with The Divine, One or Monad. Therefore, his school resembles a school of meditation or contemplation. Plotinus believed that the soul never descended into a body; it remained in the heavens, above the flesh and the physical world.[99] Plotinus by denying the soul's descent into the body, identified sensible matter as evil and the cause of the soul's confusion.

Iamblichus taught a more ritualized method of unification with the Divine, known as Theurgy, that involved invocation and religious, as well as magical, ritual. Porphyry advised the philosopher to forego all ritual activities in order to return "alone, through himself, to God alone"; while the philosopher should understand the enchantments of nature and the cults tied to its daemons, he should have nothing to do with them. "In every respect," Porphyry says, "the philosopher is the savior himself." [100] Furthermore, Porphyry maintained that permanent escape from the material was possible only for the philosopher, not for the common person. Yet, it is interesting to note that Porphyry introduced Iamblichus to Theurgy who discovered its deeper significance. Iamblichus moved Theurgy from periphery to center, not only in the life of the philosopher, but for anyone who worshipped the gods. At issue was the divinity of the world, and for Iamblichus the most effective means to acknowledge this was through the performance of rites that conformed the soul to its orders. For Porphyry, Platonism was limited to intellectual elite. The Theurgical Platonism of

---

[98] Iamblichus, 2006 translation. (p. 335)
[99] Shaw, G. 1951. (p. 10)
[100] Shaw, G. 1951. (p. 13)

Iamblichus, by contrast, allowed for gradations of religious experience that corresponded to the different levels of cosmos and society.[101] An intellectual understanding does not connect Theurgists with divine beings, for what would prevent those who philosophize theoretically from having Theurgic union with the gods? Iamblichus reasoned that it is the power of ineffable symbols alone comprehended by the Gods that establishes Theurgical union.[102] The actions performed in Theurgic rites were the work of the gods actualized by an embodied soul. Participation in this action depended entirely on the soul's suitability as a carrier of the gods- from a Theurgic perspective, the embodied soul was a receptacle of the god like the other receptacles used in Theurgic divination. As a receptacle of the gods, the soul reflected their activity and habits.

The Theurgist as creator

According to Iamblichus every human soul contains the ineffable presence of the One. It is the essential nature of the "One of the soul" to be united with the gods. Iamblichus said that the soul was capable of this unification "[because] there subsists in its very essence an innate knowledge of the gods."[103] The role of Theurgy is to awaken the soul to the presence of the One that it bore unknowingly. Theurgic ritual transforms the soul's somatic, emotional, and intellectual identity through "symbols" and "tokens" that unite the soul with the Demiurge.[104] The soul's return to the divine, therefore, demands that it ritually reenact cosmogenesis. When the soul activates the power of these symbols, their presence in the soul is awakened, for example, when meaningless names of the gods are chanted. Theurgy, like death, separates the soul from its

---

[101] Shaw, G. 1951. (p. 14)
[102] Shaw, G. 1951. (p. 84)
[103] Shaw, G. 1951. (p. 119)
[104] Shaw, G. 1951. (p. 110)

embodied identity and causes it to experience post-mortem purifications and rewards. The highest condition for souls was not their enjoyment of divine status, but their bestowal of divine measurements in cosmogenesis.

Iamblichus therefore, believed Theurgy to be an imitation of the gods, and in his major work, On the Egyptian Mysteries, he describes Theurgic observance as "ritualized cosmogony" that endows embodied souls with the divine responsibility of creating and preserving the Cosmos. Theurgical Platonism represents Iamblichus's attempt to introduce the divine mimesis of Egyptian cult to the Platonic community and the Hellenic world.[105] Theurgy imitates the gods. By sharing the activity of creation, the Theurgist would participate in the ordering of matter, which was the specific function of the Demiurge as described in Plato's *Timaues*.

The mechanism of Theurgy

Iamblichus' analysis was that the transcendent could not be grasped with mental contemplation because the transcendent is supra rational. Theurgy is a series of rituals and operations aimed at recovering the transcendent essence by retracing the divine 'signatures' through the layers of being. One's attitude to the body and matter, then, would be an index of the degree and manner of one's participation in the Demiurge. Theurgy is the dynamic expression of the mathematical mean, establishing continuity between mortal and immortal realms by allowing embodied souls to enter divine energies throughout the performance of ritual. [106]

Matter is the obstacle that keeps souls from communion with the gods. Since the gods are free from the pollution of matter,

---

[105] Shaw, G. 1951. (p. 23)
[106] Shaw, G. 1951. (p. 14)

to reach them souls must break free from material bonds. Iamblichus says:

"Just as the Gods split matter with lightning and separate from it from things which are essentially immaterial but have been dominated and bound by matter, and from being passive render them impassive, so also our fire, imitating the activity of the divine fire, destroys everything material in the sacrifices, purifies the offerings by fire, and frees them from the bonds of matter. It makes them suitable for communion with the Gods through the purity of nature and in the same manner it frees us from the bonds of generation, assimilates us to the Gods, makes us fit for their friendship, and leads our material nature up to the immaterial."

-DE MYSTERIIS 215-

Iamblichus described the human soul as the *eschatos kosmos*, the last world and reality: "Recognize, if you will, the lowest of divine beings: the soul purified from the body." Because the human soul is the lowest divinity, it suffers with the mortal lives that it sustains. Identified with only certain parts of the cosmos, the soul lost its perspective of the whole and became absorbed into the flux of mortal life. The body is connatural with the soul, the soul with the intellect and the intellect with god. Iamblichus was aware of the problems of embodiment and believed that Theurgy was able to cure souls of somatic identification by guiding them into divinely sanctioned postures. Tied to generated life, the soul is bound to laws administered by daemonic intermediaries, and until the soul achieves a proper relation with them, it remains subject to the punishments of their administration.

Iamblichus believed that certain objects (plants, animals, stones, etc.) served as receptacles of the gods because they preserved an intimate relation with them and bore their "signatures" (*sunthēmata)* in the manifest world. As such, they were pure specimens of divine presence in matter, and for souls suffering a specific imbalance within the administration of a divine being, the objects that bore its symbol *sunthēmata* became homeopathic antidotes if handled in a ritually appropriate manner. Through the appropriate use of the gods' *sunthēmata* in nature, the soul could awaken in itself the power of their corresponding symbols. [107] The *sunthēmata* of the *Chaldean Oracles* are considered as the 'thoughts of the Father' and have a cosmogonic role similar to that of the Forms in Middle Platonism; they have an anagogic function: when the soul remembers the paternal *sunthēma*, it returns to the paternal Intellect. According to Iamblichus, the gods create all things by means of images and signify all things through *sunhēmata*. Iamblichus's theoretical justification for the use of material objects in Theurgy may thus be summarized as follows:

1) The gods illuminate matter and are present immaterially in material things;
2) There exists a filial and beneficent bond between the gods who preside over life and the lives, which they produce;
3) The sacrificial order in Theurgy was connected to the order of the gods.

Yet, the *sunthēmata* embedded in nature are not limited to dense matter, but are also present in certain incantations (including melodies and rhythms), concoctions, characters traced on the earth, and the ineffable names that are able to draw souls into the presence of the gods. From a Theurgical perspective, the cosmos is a temple whose sacrificial orders were designed by the Demiurge. Union with the gods is not impossible for those whose embodiment was properly consecrated. The Theurgist is simultaneously man and god. By means of appropriate rites, the Theurgist directs the powers of his particular soul (*mikros kosmos*) into alignment with the powers of the World-Soul, which gives him direct participation

---

[107] Shaw, G. 1951. (p. 49)

in the "whole."[108] All natures are led back to the causes by which they were generated, even as far as the mundane body. For this body, being perfect, is elevated to the mundane soul, which is intellectual. However, the soul of this body is elevated to intellect, and intellect to that which is first. All things, therefore, extend themselves to this, beginning from that which is last, according to the peculiar ability of each. As a result, the magician is not only said to aspire after divinity, but also to enjoy him as far as possible. [109]

Divine possession

"But the presence of the Gods, indeed, imparts to us health of body, virtue of soul, purity of intellect, and in one word elevates everything in us to its proper principle.... In addition to these things, also, the manifestation of the Gods imparts truth and power, rectitude of works, and gifts of the greatest goods..."

-Iamblichus-

Education is important for comprehending the scheme of things as presented by Aristotle, Plato and Pythagoras, as well as by the Chaldean Oracles. The Theurgist works 'like with like': at the material level, with physical symbols and 'magic'; at the higher level, with mental and purely spiritual practices. Starting with correspondences of the divine in matter, the Theurgist eventually reaches the level where the soul's inner divinity unites with The Divine.

Iamblichus often repeats the Neoplatonic principle that "like approaches like," and in the case of a particular embodied soul the only way to reach the universality of the World and celestial souls was to become like them, that is, spherical. It is within his

---

[108] Shaw, G. 1951. (p. 51)
[109] Iamblichus, 2006 translation. (p. 226)

spherical vehicle that the Theurgist receives visions and is unified with the gods. Furthermore, the Theurgist has to purify the future vehicle of the god in order to receive its power, for the presence of the god is always in proportion to the purity of its receptacle. *Epitēdeiotēs* was the term Iamblichus used to describe the "fitness" or "aptitude" to receive a form. Although the gods were everywhere, their powers could not affect souls that lacked an appropriate receptacle. Only when the vehicle was prepared could divine possession occur. It is the purity of the receiving soul- not the geographical placing- that allows for divine possessions, including those experienced privately by every Theurgist. [110]

The meaning of Theurgy in the history of Platonism becomes clear if it is seen as the praxis that allows souls to move from the experience of the embodiment as an isolated prison to a participation in the World-Soul, where its particularity is reestablished in the unity of the whole. By entering into the community of the gods as one of its bodies of light, the embodied soul is no longer alienated by matter not passionately drawn to it. Embodiment is transformed from the psychic chaos of suffering into a cosmos, and adornment of the divine. The "lapse of time" in the *Timaeus* (30a) between material chaos and cosmos- though only a necessity of discourse when speaking of the World-Soul- is an accurate description of the experience of the embodied soul on its path to demiurgy. In Theurgy the soul gradually transforms the chaos of its embodied experience into the perfect measures of the cosmos. For Iamblichus, matter was the index that measured the degrees of divinity, and for particular souls, their relation to matter also determined the kind of Theurgy they were to practice. In imitation of divine beings, the Theurgist becomes a vehicle throught which the gods appeared to the physical world and through which he receives their communion.

---

[110] Shaw, G. 1951. (p. 87)

Iamblichus says that Theurgy does not act through the intellect but through one's entire character to allow the soul to exchange one life for another, to sacrifice its mortal life for the life of a god. Theurgy transforms the soul by conforming it to the divine actions communicated in Theurgic symbols: the sacred stones, plants, animals, prayers, and names that "preserve the will of the gods." Theurgic *noēsis* is, in fact, the act of a god knowing itself through the activity and the medium of the soul, not vice versa. *Noēsis,* in fact, was not conceptual, and Iamblichus maintained that noetic contacts with the gods are more erotic than intellectual. Theurgy successfully embodies this desire in proportion to the soul's capacity to homologize itself to the cosmos.

The ascent to the One is not possible unless the soul coordinates itself to the All and, with the All, moves itself toward the universal principle of all things.

"But by how much the higher we ascend, and elevate ourselves to the sameness both in form and essence, of first natures, and proceed from parts to wholes, by so much the more shall we discover the union which has an eternal existence, and survey the essence, which has a precedaneous and more principal subsistence, and possesses about, and in itself, difference and multitude."

-Iamblichus-

According to Pythagorean teachings, the One manifests itself as a coordinated multiplicity: a Whole, and similarly, the "One in the soul" manifests itself when the soul ritually coordinates its multiplicity into a whole. Iamblichus believed that the unifying power principle that transforms the soul in Theurgy was the same principle that held the cosmos together as its universal *philia* or *erōs.* A single friendship contains all things and produces this unifying bond by means of ineffable communion.

In short, *philia* sustained both the cosmos and every act of Theurgy. Erōs coordinates the Ideas in the intelligible world and, proceeding with them, knitted the cosmos together in a unified bond. In a word, the will of the Demiurge was revealed as Erōs:

> *"For after he conceived his works, the Self-generated Paternal Mind sowed the bond of love, heavy with fire, into all things…. in order that the All might continue to love for an infinite time and that the things woven by intellectual light of the Father might not collapse….[It is] with this Love (erōs) that the elements of the world remain on course."* [111]

Erōs (Greek: Ἔρως), in Greek mythology, is the primordial god of lust, beauty, love, and intercourse. He was also worshipped as a fertility deity. Erōs, as a primeval deity, embodies not only the force of erotic love but also the creative urge of ever-flowing nature, the firstborn Light for the coming into being and ordering of all things in the cosmos. In Hesiod's Theogony, Erōs sprang forth from the primordial Chaos together with Gaia, the Earth, and Tartarus, the underworld. According to Aristophanes' play *The Birds* (c. 414 BC), Erōs burgeons forth from an egg laid by Nyx (Night) conceived with Erebus (Darkness). In the Eleusinian mysteries, he was worshiped as *Protogonus*, the first-born. His Roman counterpart was Cupid [desire], also known as Amor [love]. In other myths, Erōs was the son of the deities Aphrodite and Ares, but according to Plato's *Symposium* he was conceived by Poros (Plenty) and Penia (Poverty) at Aphrodite's birthday.

Although Erōs is initially felt for a person, with contemplation it becomes an appreciation of the beauty within that person, or even becomes appreciation of beauty itself. Plato does not talk of physical attraction as a necessary part of love, hence the use of the word platonic to mean, "without physical attraction." In

---

[111] Shaw, G. 1951. (p. 124)

addition, Plato also said Erōs helps the soul recall knowledge of beauty, and contributes to an understanding of spiritual truth. Lovers and philosophers are all inspired to tell the truth by Erōs. Therefore, like Dionysus, Erōs was sometimes referred to as *Eleutherios* [the liberator].

In fact, Theurgy saves the soul *and* the cosmos, for without the soul Erōs cannot arise as the "first born god," and the cosmos would never come to exist.

Symbols as ontological traces of the divine and their function in Theurgy

The symbolic attitude of ancient knowledge cultivated the intellect to the extent of perceiving all of the phenomena of nature itself as a symbolic writing revealing the forces and laws governing the energetic and even spiritual aspects of our universe.[112] By the hieratic symbolic method the aim is no longer to translate things into sensory terms, but to put ourselves into the state 'magically' identical with the symbol-object, so as to become heavy with the quality of weight, to become red with the quality of redness, to burn with the quality of fire. The symbol is thus the object, exterior to us, which awakens innate knowledge through the senses. The only way we will ever know this non-definable idea is through the certainty of our innate knowledge, which assures us of this reality, which is necessarily implied in the symbol. A method of viewing is required comparable to our hearing faculty: one must learn to *listen to the symbolic image,* allowing it to enter into and pervade one's consciousness. With the expansion of consciousness, our thought is heading towards 'direct synthetic vision.' One need only note the philosophic principles to which the symbols conform in order to learn then to seek in oneself the summary meaning of their synthesis.

---

[112] Schwaller De Lubicz, R.A. 1981

The symbol is a sign that one must learn to read, and the symbolic is a form of writing whose laws one must know; they have nothing in common with the grammatical construction of our languages. Schwaller De Lubicz proposes the following explanation:

1) The first of these forms requires the object or objectification of the concept, hence the placing of the concept in Time and Space. This form may be called the 'static intelligence,' which is also designated as 'exotericism.'

2) The other from of intelligence conceives intuitively, but without yet *formulating* the concept. This is called 'innate knowledge.' It corresponds moreover to a certain way of seeing possessed by ancient Greek philosophers. They acknowledged that inscribed in the soul was the universal knowledge that the exterior object awakens through the senses. Now, it is precisely *the consciousness of the state of this innate knowledge that can vary*, that is, progressively expand and grow richer or poorer. [113]

When an image, a collection of letters, a word or a phrase, a gesture, a single sound, a musical harmony or melody have significance through *evocation*, we are dealing with a symbol. This presupposes that the meaning of the determined aspect of the symbol must be known, to be able to evoke a non-determined aspect in the consciousness of the observer. This is the common nature of the symbol.

In general, we classify symbols as follows:

i) Exoteric symbols- all the data- symbol and evocation- are objective or objectifiable (Y.M.C.A., U.N., etc.);

ii) The esoteric symbol is different- it is of a magical nature. The esoteric symbol is a natural or artificial fact, which elicits an abstract vital response, which will then be expressed physically, nervously, mentally, or emotionally in an

---

[113] Schwaller De Lubicz, R.A. 1981

organized being, or by an energetic reaction in a non-organized being.

Esoteric means the "inner" (eso-), in the sense of the inner consciousness; the contemplative, mystical or meditative transpersonal perspective. This is something different from the ordinary everyday understanding of things, and can only be understood by intuition or higher mental or spiritual faculties.

The opposite of Esoteric is Exoteric, which means the "outer" (exo-), i.e. the outer or surface or everyday consciousness. This includes both the scientific-materialistic and the conventional (or literal) religious perspective. It is based on the everyday understanding of things, and does not require any transformation of consciousness. It assumes that the everyday mind alone can understand Reality. Central to the distinction between Esoteric and Exoteric is that of *states of consciousness*.[114]

Creation is constant for esotericism, but for exotericism, it is located: "In the beginning ….." Whether it is a natural or combined image, or a conventional sign, the property of the symbol is to be a synthesis. They serve only as support of an essentially qualitative function, which probably cannot be specified in Time and Space. Synthesis should not be considered solely as a product of thought.

A symbol does not have to be true, nor to be considered as such; it is not the truth, but it is the 'reality' that it conveys. It is objectively determined in Time and Space, but, as simultaneity (synthesis), it is outside of Time. The symbol as synthesis is the eternal 'Present Moment,' because the same conjunction of conditions that created its development will compel it continually to be what it is; this prescribed the notion of identity, which is objectively inconceivable. We are dealing here with a new consciousness, that is, epistemologically speaking, a new state of the power of thought; this seems to have been

---

[114] http://www.kheper.net/topics/esotericism/esoteric_and_exoteric.htm

known to and evident among the Ancient Egyptians, since they constructed all their expression on the knowledge of this dualism of intelligence, which tradition labels Exotericism and Esotericism.[115]

In relation to a new function, the symbol counts as One, or single unity. Thus, each part of what composes it can no longer be regarded as individuality and can no longer even be objectified. Every circle, as a circular movement, has a center. The center controls; it is *the will of the figure*. Will is esoteric; effect is exoteric. Exoterically we foresee that, under certain conditions, a given cause will produce a given result. Now, philosophically, a cause is only Cause at the moment it produces an effect, which is in no way certain. The contained will must always be sought in the symbol, when the symbol is selected for an esoteric teaching. The character of this Will is that which will always compel Spirit- non-polarized Energy- to define itself in Time and Space, hence in the *form* of the symbol. This is the 'magical' meaning of the symbol. The cause, apparently outside the system, is in it, eternally united and present, and creation is constant. Such-and-such a phenomenon was not; it is always in our innate knowledge, from which our consciousness increasingly expands with experience. [116]

Metaphysical symbols show the bodiless by means of bodies. Moreover, the symbol is anagogic, serving as a ladder to ascent to the divine. Divine symbols have a transformative and elevating power. They are woven into the very fabric of Being; directly attached and unified to the gods, which are themselves the symbolic principles of being. What is important is the underlying theological and cosmological conception of the divine principles and powers that appear and become visible through certain images, things, numbers, sounds, omens, or other traces of presence.[117]

---

[115] Schwaller De Lubicz, R.A. 1981
[116] Schwaller De Lubicz, R.A. 1981
[117] Uždavinys, A. 2008 (I)

The iconoclastic Amarna theology, established in Egypt during the reign of Akhenaten (1352 – 1338 B.C.), sought to abolish mythical imagery; yet even in this theology, the sun-disc, Aten, is the One in whom millions live; the Light of Aten creates everything and by seeing this light, the eye is created. Although the Aten is attested as a god prior to Akhenaten's reign, Akhenaten's institution of the cult of the Aten as sole deity is unique in the history of Egyptian religion. What he did was to single out this god—who was manifest in the sun disk and its radiating rays of sunlight—from among the others, to be the object of veneration. The Aten was the sun god, and the solar disk was the form in which this divinity appeared. In fact, over the course of Akhenaten's reign one can trace a development that reflects the king's role in implementing a radical new theology. Although other deities were initially still recognized, Akhenaten soon ordered the abrogation of their cults; the persecution of traditional deities, particularly those of Thebes, intensified, as the name and representation of the god Amun were expunged from monuments throughout the land. Even the plural word for "gods" was frequently erased. The king, who had earlier dropped the name Amenhotep in favor of Akhenaten, had the didactic name of the Aten revised so that it no longer contained elements suggestive of polytheism.

The hieratic realities articulated by the ineffable (or esoteric) symbols and tokens of the gods are none other than the 'divine words' that constitute the entire visible world. If the universe is a manifestation of divine principles, as the Egyptian term *kheperu* indicates, then all manifested noetic and material entities are nothing but the multiform images, symbols and traces of the ineffable One shining through the intellective rays of *deus revelatus*, the demiurgic Intellect. The gods create everything by means of representations (images which reflect their noetic archetypes) and establish the hidden 'thoughts' of the original source of all things, or One, through the symbolic traces or tokens that are intelligible only to the gods themselves and have the uplifting *heka* power, to say it in the Egyptian terms. *Heka* literally means *activating the Ka*. *Heka* implied great power and influence, particularly in the case of drawing upon the Ka of the gods in a ritual manner. Heka acted together with *Hu*, the principle of divine utterance, and *Sia*, the concept of divine omniscience, to create the basis of creative power both in the mortal world and the world of the gods. It is therefore said, that the image marks the material world in its status as a fainter reproduction of a higher principle, but the world seen as symbol indicates its status as a manifestation-that is, something that works according to the logic of the trace, with the capacity to point us back up to the higher orders that produced it. [118]

Sumbola and *sunthémata*, understood in the particular metaphysical sense, are not arbitrary signs, but ontological traces of the divine, inseparable from the entire body of manifestation: the cosmos, as the revealed divine *agalma* (statue or shrine), is itself the Symbol *par excellence* of the noetic realm and its Creator. It represents that which is above representation and is an imminent receptacle of the transcendent principles. Therefore, the demiurgic Logos is both the sower and distributor of all ontological symbols or, rather, symbols constitute its manifested totality and these symbols, when gathered, awakened, re-kindled, lead up to the noetic and supra-noetic reality. The One is the origin of all things. The One created as an intermediary the "maker"- the *demiourgos* (demiurge or *nous*) also called the Word (Logos), which is a perfect image of the One and the archetype of all existing things. It is at once being and thought, ideal world and idea. The *sumbola* should therefore be conceived as passwords or tokens in the soul's ritual ascent. What is really at issue here is the manner by which the ritual accomplishment (*telesiourgia*) of ineffable acts and the mysterious power of the unspeakable symbols allow us to re-establish the Theurgic union with the gods. The ascent through invocations, symbolic contemplations, and rites, results in revelation of the blessed sights and activity, which is no longer human.

---

[118] Uždavinys, A. 2008 (I)

The Greek term *sumbolon* (derived from the verb *sumballein*, meaning 'to join') initially denoted a half of a whole object, such as *tessera hospitalis*, which could be joined with the other half in order that the two contracting parties- or members of a secret brotherhood- might have proof of their identity. A symbol therefore only appears and becomes significant when two parties make an intentional rupture of the whole, or when the One manifests itself as plurality, that is when Osiris or Dionysus is rendered asunder. In this original sense, the symbol 'reveals its meaning by the fact that one of its halves fits in with or corresponds to the other.' [119] When viewed in accordance to the 'vertical' metaphysical asymmetry, one half of imagined *tessera hospitalis* represents the visible things (the symbol proper) and another half stands for the invisible noetic or supra-noetic reality symbolized by the lower visible part. The initiation and spiritual ascent consists in joining these two separate parts. That means re-uniting the manifested *sumbolon* (as a trace) and the hidden principle, which is thereby 'symbolized.'

The 'symbolic life' is the life of knowledge, which enables one's recollection, reintegration and return to the 'original source.' The process of transformation, *sakhu*, literally means 'making an *akh*.' The *akh* is associated with thought, but not as an action of the mind; rather, it was intellect as a living entity. The *akh* was the immortal part, the radiant and shining being that lived on in the Sahu, the intellect, will and intentions of the deceased that transfigured death and ascended to the heavens to live with the gods or the imperishable stars. Those deceased who have become *akhu* can still act for or against the living, and exist with them in a reciprocal relationship. If the living care and maintain the deceased, the deceased can care and protect the living. The *akhu* came in to being after the deceased passed judgment after death, and the *ka** and *ba*[#] united. This

---

*Ka (corporal presence/life force): The *ka* was the concept of life force, the difference between a living and a dead person, death

---

[119] Uždavinys, A. 2008 (II)

ritualized transformation is designated as 'going forth by day' from the Duat into the intelligible 'day' of Ra and appearing as Ra. Thereby one's *ba* (as a symbol) is made *akh*-effective in the Isle of Fire (which is the solar realm of the Platonic Forms). The Theurgic texts to be ritually recited as a means of ascent themselves are regarded as *akhu* that are 'pleasing to the heart of Ra.' The ultimate goal of this 'symbolic wisdom' is to make the Eye of Horus sound and whole, that is, to restore one's primordial 'golden' nature, like the pure mirror (*ankh*) which reflects the intelligible light of Ra and is 'sacrificially' reintegrated into the realm of *akhu*.[120]

In the context of the Hellenic Mysteries and Orphic-Pythagorean tradition, the symbol may be a deity's secret name, an omen or

---

occurring when the *ka* left the body. The Ka was thought to be created by Khnum on a potter's wheel, or passed on to children via their father's semen. The Egyptians also believed that the *ka* was sustained through food and drink. For this reason food and drink offerings were presented to the dead, though it was the *kau* within the offerings (also known as *kau*) that was consumed, not the physical aspect. The *ka* was often represented in Egyptian iconography as a second image of the individual, leading earlier works to attempt to translate *ka* as double.

#**Ba (soul/personality):** The *ba* is in some regards the closest to the Western notion of the soul, but it also was everything that makes an individual unique, similar to the notion of personality. (In this sense, inanimate objects could also have a *ba*, a unique character, and indeed Old Kingdom pyramids were often called the ba of their owner). Like a soul, the *ba* is a part of a person that lives after the body dies, and it is sometimes depicted as a human-headed bird flying out of the tomb to join with the ka in the afterlife. As with humans, deities could also have a *ba*, but in the case of divine beings, it was even more associated with their impressiveness, power, and reputation. When a god intervened in human affairs, it was said that the *bau* (plural of *ba*) of the god where at work. In this regard, the king was regarded as a *ba* of a god, or one god was believed to be the *ba* of another.

---

[120] Uždavinys, A. 2008 (II)

a cultic formula. These symbols allow the initiate to pass into the realm of the gods like the Egyptian pharaoh who takes the night-journey 'as the representative of all human beings' and sails through the Netherworld with the *Ba* of Ra in the solar bark. The acquired Apollonian wisdom enables one to perceive the hidden divine 'thoughts,' the immaterial archetypes, or Ideas. Hellenic writers correctly maintained that symbols are especially an Egyptian mode of imitating the demiurgic activity of the gods.

The Neoplatonists maintain that the lowest things are in the highest and the highest things are in the lowest. In the depths of its own nature, each manifested thing keeps the mysterious and hidden symbol of the universal 'Father.' By means of Theurgical rites the soul is purified, transformed, and conducted to the divine realm, as if carried 'on the wings of Thoth.' The vindicated soul is separated from the mortal receptacle and re-united with the noetic principles. Separation, purification, and elevation to the realm of eternal, noetic 'day' (as well as subsequent return to the ineffable One) is regarded as the existential and metaphysical rite of 'homecoming,' during which the initiate buries his body with the exception of the head. The head is not buried, because the soul, which abides in it does not undergo 'death.' This sacramental act has an additional peculiar feature: it is the initiate who at the binding of the Theurgists buries his own body. [121]

The Theurgist purifies both the body, as material receptacle of the divine rays, and the soul, as the immortal divine seed or the winged bird detached from the inanimate body and the related psycho-somatic self-consciousness. As the *Pyramid Texts* say: '*ba* to heaven, *shat* (body in the sense of corpse) to earth.' Eventually, the Theurgist worships 'The Lord of All' (*neb tem*). Unification is possible, because 'The Lord of All' has sown the secret symbols in the soul (according to Proclus). When these essentially hidden symbols are remembered, re-awakened, and

---

[121] Uždavinys, A. 2008 (II)

re-sounded, the soul, mythically speaking, returns through the fiery ray to its noetic and supra-noetic Principle. However, esoterically, we might say that 'God' returns to 'God,' even if, ultimately, this return is only a sort of divine dream, or illusion, when viewed from the point of the all-embracing, ineffable God himself.

In essence, the Theurgic symbols do not merely represent invisible and divine things, but are inherently connected with them: in a sense, they 'are' the gods. The symbol of the transcendent One, hidden in the soul, is regarded as the essential henadic aspect of the soul (called the 'one of the soul') by which the mystical union with the One is realized. At the lower levels of reality, the *sunthémata* function as receptacles for the gods (for their *bau*), because 'the gods illuminate matter and are present immaterially in material things. Even spices, aromatics, sounds, and numbers may serve as the proper receptacles for the anagogic divine powers. The Demiurge and his assistant *neteru* themselves determine and conduct the Theurgic rites that put the soul into correspondence and *sustasis* is often applied to the prayer/ invocation (*logos*) which affects conjunction. [122]

In conclusion, a god does not literally dwell on earth in his cultic receptacles, but rather installs himself there, thereby 'animating' the images and symbols. It is the *ba* (manifestation, noetic and life-giving power, descending 'soul') that is somewhat united with the cult statues. The divine *ba* can permeate the human body as well, thereby confirming the latter's ability to participate in the superior principles. The Platonic philosopher, like the bird-shaped *ba* of the Egyptian initiate, indeed must re-grow his wings in order to fly up to the stars (visible symbols of the eternal noetic archetypes) and, standing on the back of the ouroboric universe, to contemplate what lies beyond and what is, therefore, formless and colorless. Neither the outward, nor the inward psychic seer is capable of

---

[122] Uždavinys, A. 2008 (II)

seeing without images. The nature of the things seen, in each case, corresponds to the nature and preparedness of the seer himself, that is, to the particular archetypal measures or configurations and to the actual contents of his existential and culturally shaped consciousness. [123]

God- the Monad or First Principle- and the gods

"For every God first exhibits the peculiarity of his presence with secondary natures in himself; because he imparts himself to other things also according to his own exuberant plenitude."

-Proclus-

The "Pythagorean" Monad is All encompassing. The Monad is above all other Gods. He is the unthinkable, outside the realm of any definition. The God who is the cause of generation, of all nature, and of all the powers in the elements, as transcending these, and as being immaterial, incorporeal, and supernatural, unbegotten and impartible, wholly derived from himself, and concealed in himself, - this God precedes all things, and comprehends all things in Himself.[124] He is established as the paradigm of the God who is the father of Himself, since he has no other origin. It is the principle which produces all Being. For this reason, the Neoplatonists thought that the One could not itself be a being. If it were a being, it would have a particular nature, and so could not be universally productive of all being. Because it is *beyond being*, it is also beyond thought, because thinking requires the determinations which belong to being: the division between subject and object, and the distinction of one thing from another. This God is all things causally and is able to affect all things. He likewise does produce all things, yet, not by himself alone, but in conjunction with those divine powers,

---

[123] Uždavinys, A. 2008 (I)
[124] Iamblichus, 2006 translation. (p.285)

which continually germinate, as it were, from him, as from a perennial root. Not that he is in want of these powers to the efficacy of his productive energy, but the universe requires their cooperation, in order to the distinct subsistence of its various parts and different forms. For as the *essence* of the first cause, if it be lawful so to speak, is full of deity, his immediate energy must be deific, and his first progeny must be gods [as we know them]. However, as he is ineffable and superessential, all things proceed from him ineffably and superessentially.[125] This Ineffable One is therefore, the God of gods, a Monad from the One, prior to essence, and in the principle of essence. For from him entity and essence are derived. The One causes things to exist by donating unity, and the particular manner in which a thing is one is its form. As the One confers individuality it is in reality the principle of plurality.

When dealing with the ineffable, we are never able to describe that reality itself. But we can understand the dynamics of the Godhead by analogy with the created realities, such as the gods, which are in a sense the first manifestations of the unmanifest. According to Proclus, every soul is composed of *noeroi logoi* (intellective reason principles) and *theia sumbola* (divine symbols). The former are related with the intelligible Forms, reflected or manifested at the level of soul, and, consequently, with Nous; the latter, with the divine henads or fundamental supra-noetic unities, and the One itself. For Proclus, the One (*to hen*) is God, and the multiplicity of gods is the multiplicity of self-complete henads. This particular characteristic of Proclus' system implies insertion of a level of individual ones, the *henads,* between the One itself and the divine Intellect, which is the second principle. Yet, Proclus also argues that there are two orders of henads, one consisting of self-complete principles, the other of irradiations from them. These irradiations are like the Egyptian *bau* that constitute the descending divine series whose members (*bau*) appear at different levels of reality. They may be

---

[125] Iamblichus, 2006 translation. (p. 166)

designated as symbols that function as a means of transformative ascent and re-union of the soul (itself regarded as the *ba* in the multiple sequence of divine *bau*). In this sense, the word *ba* means any noetic and psychic 'manifestation' (as an image or symbol of some higher principle), imbued with being, life, and intelligence, albeit in different degrees of proportions. In the descending chain of theogony, cosmogony, and demiurgic irradiation, for instance, Ra (the solar *Nous*) is the manifested *ba* of the ineffable Principle, Sekhmet is the *ba* of Ra, Bastet is the *ba* of Sekhmet, and every living cat is the *ba* of Bastet. [126]

"Gods should be iridescent, like the rainbow in the storm. Man creates a God in his own image, and the gods grow old along with the men that made them. But storms sway in heaven, and the god-stuff sways high and angry over our heads. Gods die with men who have conceived them. But the god-stuff roars eternally, like the sea, with too vast a sound to be heard."

-D.H. Lawrence, The Plumed Serpent-

The Gods [as a product of the Monad] are self-perfect superessential unities, so far as they are gods. For the principal subsistence of everything is according to the summit of its essence, and this in the Gods is The One, or Monad, through which they are profoundly united to each other and to The One itself, or the ineffable principle of things, from which they are ineffably unfolded into light. All these Gods are in, and profoundly united to, each other, and their union is far greater than the communion and sameness, which subsist in beings. [127]

Some of the gods are characterized by permanency, others by progression, and others by conversion, or regression. Some are universal, others more particular. Some, again, are generative, others anagogic, or of an elevating nature, and others

---

[126] Uždavinys, A. 2008 (II)
[127] Iamblichus, 2006 translation. (p. 348)

demiurgic; and universally, there are different characteristics of different Gods (the connective, perfective, demiurgic, assimilative, etc.).

PART III

PRAXIS

"Knowledge of the Gods is accompanied with a conversion to, and the knowledge of, ourselves"

-Iamblichus-

Theurgy is cosmogonic activity, a mimesis of the gods in creation. It is not thinking that connects Theurgists to the gods, but ineffable acts. If, as the Platonists maintain, god is always doing geometry, then the Theurgist is his instrument. Yet, "it is not possible for any of the divine actions to be performed in a sacred manner without one of the Superior Beings present to oversee and complete the sacred acts." [128]

The gods, Iamblichus says, were everywhere, but they could be received only by a vehicle that had been properly prepared. Iamblichus distinguishes three types of human souls:

1) The great herd that follow nature and fate;
2) Those that have risen to the divine Nous above nature and fate;
3) Those that are between the two extremes.

To each type of soul, there is a corresponding mode of worship. Souls governed by the nature of the universe, leading lives according to their own personal nature and using the powers of nature, should perform their worship in a manner adapted to nature and to the corporeal things moved by nature. In their worship they should employ places, climates, matter and the powers of matter, bodies and their characteristics and qualities, movements and what follows movements, and changes of the things in generation, along with other things associated with these in their acts of reverence to the gods, and especially in the part that pertains to performing sacrifice. Other souls, living according to the *Nous* alone and the life of the *Nous*, and liberated from the bonds of nature, should concern themselves in all parts of Theurgy with the intellectual and incorporeal law of the hieratic art. Other souls, the media between these, should labor along different paths of holiness according to the

---

[128] Iamblichus, 2006 translation. (p. 144)

differences in their intermediate position, either by participating in both modes of ritual worship, or by separating themselves from one mode, or by accepting both of these as a foundation for more honorable things- for without them the transcendent gods would never be reached." [129]

In technical terms, we refer to these different modes as:

1) material sunthēmata;
2) intermediate sunthēmata; and
3) noetic sunthēmata.

Encosmic gods are responsible for the material order and should receive material offerings, hypercosmic gods receive noetic gifts, and the intermediate gods receive both, or a mixture of, or one in favor of, the other. The correspondence between Iamblichus's theology, psychology, and ritual worship is summarized in *Table 2*.

Table 2

Souls	Purposes for Embodiment	Rituals	Gods
Material	For punishment and judgment	Material	Encosmic/ material
Intermediate	To exercise and correct moral habits	Immaterial and material	Intermediate: joining encosmic to hypercosmic
Noetic	To save, perfect, and purify generated life	Completely immaterial and noetic	Hypercosmic/ immaterial

---

[129] Iamblichus, 2006 translation. (p. 224-225)

Since material gods are revealed by daemons, material rites necessarily work with daemonic orders, and since these same daemons rule over bodily instincts and passions, the rituals that establishes the proper measures for associating with them, also stabilizes the passions of the soul. The affections that enslaved souls to daemons has to be purified and aligned with sunthēmata in nature before the soul could reach the simpler and more unified levels of the gods. Without this collaboration with the daemons the soul lacks the foundation necessary to homologize itself to the material gods.[130] Noetic worship is useless without this foundation. Beginning with material rites the soul uses material sunthēmata as a foundation, for intermediate rites intermediate sunthēmata, and these, in turn, support the complete alignment of the soul into the order of the World-Soul in the final state.[131] In addition, the soul cannot rise to the "paternal Demiurge" alone, but has to be assimilated to the Whole, and this is accomplished only by honoring "all the gods."

The most marked transition in the progress of the soul is the rare moment that it receives a god as a guardian to replace its personal daemon. This privilege is reserved for very few souls. The great majority were best served simply by fulfilling the dictates of their guardian daemons. There are no evil daemons competing for control over the soul. The soul has only one ruling daemon and he is good. However, the soul first has to recognize him and then develop a rapport. This daemon stays there until its "limits" have been realized by the soul and a higher god replaces him. The process unites us with the gods. Eventually, we become one with the One, which is the highest of all, the most sublime and irreducible.

It is suggested that the magician makes use of all three levels of rituals, beginning with the lower form (material sunthēmata). Simplicius and Epictetus warns *"that as if you take away letters*

---

130 Shaw, G. 1951. (p. 156)
131 Shaw, G. 1951. (p. 159)

from a sentence, or change them, the form of the sentence no longer remains, thus also in divine works or words, if anything is deficient, or is changed, or is confused, divine illumination does not take place, but the indolence of him who does this dissolves the power of what is affected." Proclus furthermore states "*the [resultant] anger of the Gods does not refer any passion to them, but indicates our inaptitude to participate of them.*"

Meditation plays an important role in Theurgy and it is proper to discuss a few particulars concerning it, as it renders perfect the science concerning the gods. Meditation produces an indissoluble and sacred communion with the gods. The first form of meditation is *collective* and is the primary form to establish contact with and gain knowledge of, divinity. The second form is the *bond of concordant communion*, calling forth, prior to the energy of speech, the gifts imparted by the gods, and perfecting the whole of our operations prior to our intellectual conceptions. The third and almost perfect form of meditation is the *seal of ineffable union with the divinities,* in whom it establishes all the power and authority of meditation; and thus causes the soul to repose in the gods, as in a never failing port. However, in these three terms, in which all the divine measures are contained, suppliant adoration not only conciliates to us the friendship of the gods, but also supernally extends to us three fruits, being as it were three Hesperian apples of gold. The *first* of these pertains to *illumination*; the *second*, to a *communion of operation*; but through the energy of the *third*, we receive *a perfect plenitude of divine fire.* No operation, however, in sacred concerns, can succeed without the intervention of meditation. Lastly, the continual exercise of meditation nourishes the vigor of our intellect, and renders the receptacles of the soul far more capacious for the communications of the Gods. It likewise is the divine key, which opens to men the penetralia of the gods. Besides this, it produces an indissoluble communion and friendship with divinity, nourishes a divine love, and inflames the divine part of the soul. [132]

---

[132] Iamblichus, 2006 translation. (p. 272)

Background

> *"Immaterial beings are present in material natures*
> *immaterially"*

"The inexpressible is expressed through ineffable symbols." [133] This describes a cosmogonic and hieratic function of sunthēmata. Iamblichus says that the gods use the cosmogonic power of Daemons to reveal their will through natural signs.[134] He then explains further:

> *"The Gods produce signs by means of nature which serves them*
> *in the work of generation, nature as a whole and individual*
> *natures specifically, or by means of the generative Daemones*
> *who, presiding over the elements of the cosmos, particular*
> *bodies, animals, and everything in the world, easily produce the*
> *phenomena in whatever way seems good to the Gods. They*
> *reveal the intentions of the God symbolically."* [135]

The sunthēmata and symbols of Theurgy functions in a manner similar to Plato's Forms in that both reveal the divine order. The sunthēmata are described as the material causes implanted in the essence of souls by the Demiurge for their recollection of the gods who made them and of other [divine] things.[136] Common to Beauty and to Theurgic sunthēmata is the erōs (friendship) that initiates the soul's divination. This friendship is

---

[133] Iamblichus, 2006 translation. (p. 65)
[134] Shaw, G. 1951. (p. 163)
[135] Iamblichus, 2006 translation. (p. 135-136)
[136] Timaeus, I, 213:16-18

what binds all things together. [137] Although every soul is created by the Demiurge with "harmonic ratios" and "divine symbols," the former is active in all souls by virtue of cosmogenesis while the latter remains inactive until awakened in Theurgy. [138] To ensure the effectiveness of the rite the objects have to be fitting to the god invoked and to the material attachment of the soul. These collections form "receptacles" for the gods and Iamblichus says that Theurgists create them with "stones," "herbs," "animals," "aromatics," and other sanctified objects that possess intimate affiliations with the gods invoked, or Theurgic contact would not be effected. The horizontal sympathy that the soul shares with a symbol becomes the foundation through which its vertical power is received [from the gods].

Practice

Since the material gods are revealed by daemons, material rites necessarily work with daemonic orders, and since these same daemons rule over bodily instincts and passions, the rituals that established the proper measures for associating with them stabilize the passions of the soul.

A proper example of material sunthēmata is the erection of phalli, which is a sunthēma of generative powers, and we believe it is an act that calls out for the fecundation of cosmic genesis. This practice is also known as "Linga," as used by the Hindu culture to worship the creative powers of Shiva. Many phalli are consecrated in the spring, because then the whole world receives from the Gods the power which is productive of all generation. [139]

---

[137] Iamblichus, 2006 translation. (p. 56)
[138] Shaw, G. 1951. (p. 165)
[139] Iamblichus, 2006 translation. (p. 53)

In Egyptian lore, the phallus is associated with Osiris. In traditional Greek mythology, Hermes, god of boundaries and exchange (popularly the *messenger* god) was considered to be a phallic deity by association with representations of him on herms (pillars) featuring a phallus. There is no scholarly consensus on this depiction and it would be speculation to consider Hermes a type of fertility god. Pan, son of Hermes, was often depicted as having an exaggerated erect phallus. Also, Priapus, son of Aphrodite and either Dionysus or Adonis, was a Greek god of fertility whose symbol was an exaggerated phallus. He was the protector of livestock, fruit plants, gardens, and male genitalia. His name is the origin of the medical term priapism. Freud remarks that all elongated objects, such as sticks, tree trunks, and umbrellas (the opening of the last being comparable to an erection), may stand for the male organ. Other examples could include mountains, tall buildings, trains, pens or bananas and can be used as objects in this rite.

In contrast to the creation of a phallus, the adoration of female genitalia is generally known as *Yoni*, a Sanskrit word that means "source or origin of life." The original meaning of yoni was "Divine Passage." A child was considered to be born from a yoni of stars - constellations that prevailed during the childbirth. The Aryans had identified some 50,000 astrological yonis that favor a child's birth. Anything that can be entered, that is concealed, or resembles the vulva and/or vagina in any way is symbolic of female sexuality- for instance valleys, caves, doorways, boxes, drawers, cupboards, fruits such as figs, or flowers such as roses. Female breasts are suggested by curving or round shapes, for instance domed buildings, rolling hills or any round fruit such as gourds or melons.

As part of the rite, obscenities should be uttered. These obscenities uttered indicate the privation of beauty in matter and of the antecedent state of deformity in things about to be brought into cosmic order. Estranged from its own divinity, the soul- like chaotic matter- is also deprived of beauty, and the obscenities shouted in the rite allows the soul to recognize its ugliness apart from the divine. The soul yearns proportionately more as it despises more the ugliness in itself. This recognition awakens the soul's desire for the divine, and the erect phallus- as sunthēmata- is an image of that desire.[140; 141]

Statues of Priapus were often hung with signs bearing obscene epigrams, collected in Priapeia (treated below), which threatened sexual assault towards transgressors of the boundaries that he protected:

Percidere, puer, moneo; futuere, puella; barbatum furem tertia poena manet.

[I warn you, boy, you will be screwed; girl, you will be fucked; a third penalty awaits the bearded thief.]

Femina si furtum faciet mihi virve puerve, haec cunnum, caput hic praebeat, ille nates.

[If a woman steals from me, or a man, or a boy, let the first give me her cunt, the second his head, the third his buttocks.]

Per medios ibit pueros mediasque puellas mentula, barbatis non nisi summa petet.

[My dick will go through the middle of boys and the middle of girls, but with bearded men it will aim only for the top.] [142]

The participant does not literally worship the phallus but the divine power of fecundation. The erect phallus functions as an intermediary to the divine, a sunthēmata of the gods. The male and female sexuality are expressions of deeper creative forces, referred to by Freud as the "animus" and "anima." The animus represents the male or rational side of the psyche, and the anima the female intuitive, side.

---

[140] Shaw, G. 1951. (p. 168)
[141] Iamblichus, 2006 translation. (p. 39)
[142] Williams, C.A. 1999. (p. 21)

"Let him, before beginning his Work, endeavor to map out his own being, and arrange his invocations in such a way as to redress the balance."

-Aleister Crowley-

Background

Intermediate sunthēmata are the visible and audible sunthēmata that Iamblichus described in *De Mysteriis* as hieratic characters, symbols, names, and musical compositions. The symbolic vehicle for the soul's purification has to be suited to the specific needs of that soul, and if the soul is ready for contact with the intermediate gods, it calls for rites and sunthēmata of an intermediate order. These include characters and symbols that correspond to the planetary gods.

The visible "characters" of the planetary gods invoked in Theurgic ritual has their audible (invocative) counterparts. In general, there are three main methods of invoking any Deity:

1. The First Method consists of devotion to that deity;
2. The Second Method is the straightforward ceremonial invocation, as described in the Goetia;
3. The Third Method is Dramatic.

The Third Method is perhaps the most attractive of all. Certainly is so to the artist's temperament, for it appeals to his imagination through his aesthetic sense. [143]

Theurgists apply the following criteria for composing invocation:

1. Find out what powers and effects any particular star has in itself, what positions and aspects, and what these remove

---

[143] Crowley, A., Desti, M. and Waddell, L. 2008. (p. 145)

and produce. Detest in your lyrics what the stars remove and approve what they produce;

2. Consider which star chiefly rules, which place and man. Then observe what modes these regions and persons generally use, so that you may apply similar ones, together with the meaning first mentioned, to the word, which you wish to offer to this same star;

3. The daily positions and aspects of the stars are to be noticed; then investigate to what speech, songs, movements, dances, moral behavior and actions most men are usually incited under those aspects, so that you may make every effort to imitate these in your songs, which will agree with the similar disposition of the heavens and enable you to receive a similar influx from them. [144]

It is important to note that invocations are not attempts to compel the gods, but allow men to "imitate them" and share in their divine activity. Invocations do not, in fact, "invoke" the gods or call them down. On the contrary, they "evoke" the divine sunthēmata lying in the human soul. *"Invocation makes the intelligence of men fit to participate in the Gods, elevates it to the Gods, and harmonizes it with them through orderly persuasion."* [145] Iamblichus says the names of the gods were impressed on souls before birth and that Theurgic chants awakened them.

It is necessary to remove all conceptions and logical deductions from the divine names, and to remove as well the physical imitations of the voice naturally akin to the things in nature. Iamblichus says that even if it is unknowable to us, *"this very thing is its most venerable aspect."* In Egypt, the priests, when singing hymns in praise of the gods, employed the seven vowels, which they utter in due succession. [146] Iamblichus believed that the seven vowels were connatural with the seven

---

[144] Shaw, G. 1951. (p. 174)
[145] Iamblichus, 2006 translation. (p. 42)
[146] Shaw, G. 1951. (p. 185)

planetary gods, and certain Gnostic writings suggest that one-to-one correlations were ritually developed. Since these sounds resonate with the gods, when the soul enchanted them, it imitates the activity and the will of the Demiurge in creation. Since the soul itself cannot grasp or initiate Theurgy, the incantation, strictly speaking, is accomplished by the god, yet it frees the soul by allowing it to actively experience what it could never conceptually understand. [147] In an incantation, the Theugist becomes a citizen of two worlds. Insofar as the Theurgist becomes divine, he also commands the daemons who serve the gods, yet he does not command them as a man but as one of the gods.

Rationale

"As, therefore, the Gods generate all things through forms, in a similar manner they signify all things through signs, impressed as it were by a seal... The Gods, therefore, produce the signs, either through nature, which is subservient both generally and particularly to the generation of effects; or through genesiurgic daimons, who presiding over the elements of the universe, partial bodies, and everything contained in the world, conduct with facility the phenomena, conformably to the will of the Gods."

-Iamblichus-

The Pythagoreans apply symbols and sounds as a method of Intermediate Sunthēmata. Proclus, in his commentary on the *Timaeus*, says the chi (*X*), was the character or shape most evocative for recollecting the divination of the world and our souls. The characters mentioned by Iamblichus probably included this *X* and other symbols that corresponded to the

---

[147] Shaw, G. 1951. (p. 187)

planetary gods. The symbols were carved on walls, or reflected against walls and served as symbols for contemplation and meditation.

In this rite, we approach man as a creator of his universe, or anthropocosmic entity. We apply cosmic symbols that we can use to relate the creation of the universe to man. We then draw from the powers associated with the different planets within our own solar system, which is the same that reside within the psyche of the magician. It is believed that every aspect of the human temperament- from love to bellicosity, from lawfulness to anarchy- had its embodiment within these planets. It is important to remember that we view the Microcosm as an exact image of the Macrocosm. It is envisaged that the process brings the magician closer to an understanding of the many facets of the psyche, which resist harmonization. As much as the magician becomes a creator of his Microcosm, he becomes a creator in the Macrocosm.

The Anthropocosmic Cosmology

Humanity stands at the brink of shifting paradigms, also described as a Ragnarok- an epochal transformation of the world. Humanity now finds itself in an era ruled by Science. The qualities of the "new paradigm" are based on a variety of descriptors, such as astrology (The Age of Aquarius), time (the conclusion of the Mayan Calendar, 2012), and anthropology (the Movement of the Earth's Kundalini and the Rise of the Female Light). These descriptors all reflect the awareness that this shift is real and in association with time, that it is already taking place.

Philosophically it is clear that the new paradigm embraces the principles very similar to that of ancient Egypt's natural philosophy from nearly five thousand years ago. A significant coincidence is that the essence translated by the available literature is primarily based on what is now known as "sacred geometry," which is a derivative of the Pythagorean philosophy, and also believed to be of Egyptian origin.[148] Geometric or Number Philosophy denotes a mentality and it is this mentality that seems to resurface. It is rich in symbolism that awakes the relationship that exists between man and his gods. The proportions of the human body, the nuances of consciousness, the sizes and distances of stars, planets and moons, even the creations of humankind, are all shown to reflect their origins in geometric figures and relationships.[149] It is not essentially a Left-Hand Path approach, but surely one that evokes awareness of man and his own creative role with the gods. The Modern "Anthropocosmic" cosmology is a synthesis of ancient Egyptian cosmology, and that of modern "consciousness," in which man himself plays a central role in the creation of the universe.

> *"The anthropocosmic philosophy bases all functions and measures on the crystallization or incarnation of the Cosmos in man."*
>
> -R.A Schwaller de Lubicz, The Temple of Man (Plate 24)-

In the tradition of the great physicists of the twentieth century, today's "new science" has embarked on a quest to redefine the human experience in ways reminiscent of ancient concepts: that there is no reality in the absence of observation. [150]

Schwaller de Lubicz demonstrated that the Egyptian culture represented a magnificent worldview in which science, religion, philosophy, and art were all part of a single discipline based on man's innate and intuitive knowledge of nature and creation. The Logos, the Divine Word of the beginning, is the All, or the undifferentiated state of existence that is the nature of the Self.

---

[148] Malkowski, E.F. 2007.
[149] Melchizedek, D. 2000. (Volume II)
[150] Malkowski, E.F. 2007. (p. 309)

It is what we call spiritual, and at the same time what caused the Self to become mortal. This is the cause and struggle to attain final deliverance from mortality. Life therefore, is spiritual. Yet, it is not just spiritual, but also organic, however, encompassing the physical realities of fertilization, gestation, birth, growth, maturity, aging and death. It is also cosmic, encompassing the principles of polarity, process, relationship, substantiality, and potentiality. Logos is the principle of divine origin (which is esoteric) and the manifestation of the principle in the physical (which is exoteric). The principle whose source is undefined and the manifestation of that principle together form life, as we know it.

According to Schwaller De Lubicz the Egyptian neters collectively formed a coherent thesis explaining that all nature is, itself, the essence of Man. In Neoplatonic terminology, it is through man that these neters come to life. In the philosophy we are speaking of, the essence of the human being is eternal and it is the fate of the cosmos that is determined by both the immortalized human soul and his gods.

De Lubicz coined his principle "Anthropocosm" or "Man Cosmos." In this System, the point is the One, representing the Absolute- the concept of God-, which is the mother/father of all that is. In truth, God is unknowable and undefined. It is only through the creation of Two that consciousness comes into being. Being made in God's image, Two, or Man, is that consciousness.

Schwaller de Lubicz[151] explains the following about Unity:

"One sole Truth: Indivisible Unity
One sole Reality: the Verb and its evolution in consciousness.
One sole universal morality: through Cosmic Man each is
bound to all, each is responsible for, or benefits from, the
good and evil deeds of all;
humanity is a whole united in the individual.
One sole Consciousness: Genesis.
One sole pure science: Numbers.
One sole expression: the Symbol.
One sole means: Harmony, which has its source in disorder
where the sundered parts rediscover one another,
naturally and of themselves, through affinity.
Spirit is at the beginning and the end of all form.
Form is the symbol of a function.
Wisdom is the perfect harmony of all the functions."

Religion claims that God made us. If we are made by God, and God is in all nature, then aren't we all, as an aggregate (through our consciousness), God experiencing God self? Science claims that we are made of stardust. If we really are made from the elements of stars, as science suggests, aren't we then, through our state of consciousness, simply the universe trying to understand itself? Based on all the evidence, experiential included, there is no more fitting conclusion than that Man is just as much the cause as he is the effect of the cosmos. Man's nature is the source (the abstract Cosmos or Consciousness), and the physical Cosmos (matter) is a vehicle for expression of that source, particularly as a creative and self-perceiving entity.[152]

---

[151] Schwaller de Lubicz, R.A. 1998. (p. 1021)
[152] Malkowski, E.F. 2007. (p.379)

Sacred Geometry and the Ancient Flower of Life

"Sacred Geometry is the eternal visual language wrapped around the root concepts of the manifest universe. [153] *The archetypes and icons of geometry are absolutely perfect, unchanging, and timeless realities springing directly from Gods Mind. The Universe is Vibration, and the principles of Sacred Geometry are directly correspondent to ALL wave form phenomena . . . ALL vibration. Science agrees, the Universe is Vibration, and geometry is vibration manifest on the visual, time/space planes....* Sacred Geometry defines the nature of Space and Time.... Sacred Geometry is THE ARCHITECTURE OF THE UNIVERSE."

-Charles Gilchrist-

Sacred Geometry may be understood as a worldview of pattern recognition, a complex system of religious symbols and structures involving space, time and form. According to this belief, the basic patterns of existence are perceived as sacred. By connecting with these, a person contemplates the *Mysterium Magnum*, and the *Great Design*. By studying the nature of these patterns, forms and relationships and their connections, insight may be gained into the mysteries – the laws and lore of the Universe. The Flower of Life is considered to be a symbol of sacred geometry, said to contain ancient, religious value, depicting the fundamental forms of space and time. In this sense, it is a visual expression of the connections life weaves through all humankind.

---

[153] http://www.charlesgilchrist.com

The science of "Sacred Geometry" is based on the following:

1. The Single Point or Monad is the first archetype of Sacred Geometry. It is the absolute root mental concept . . . the simplest idea possible and directly related to "unity consciousness" or Oneness . . . undivided God-Mind. The Single Point represents the First Dimension. It is both omnipresent and omnipotent. Here Unity represents the root of all-holistic thinking- *"The All is One" and "The One is All."*

2. The two-dimensional Universe begins with the division of the Single Point. The Single Point that divides and becomes Two, represents the great and profound mystery of Sacred Geometry. Even though Sacred Geometry does not investigate beyond effect, it is accepted that the Universe is created by division- "This is the great miracle and mystery of All."

The Second Dimension literally begins at the conceptual level of "The Two Points." Formation of these two points marks the first architectural relationship of the Universe, simultaneously creating the first abstract unit of measure, i.e. space. The tremendous energies contained within this first two-dimensional relationship of the Universe manifests as two different types of motion: movement from Point A to Point B, that is linear motion (with the formation of a line), as well as circular motion of the resultant line (with the formation of a circle). This dual movement establishes the Radius and Arc of the circle. It is the root motion, or conceptual Big Bang, the Creative Unity of this System.

All the various energies of the universe trace back to the actual relationship between the Radius and the Arc (or Pi, π) of the circle. The Radius and Arc represents Duality: Yin and Yang, Light and Dark, Left and Right, East and West, Up and Down, Mother and Father. All manifestations of Two traces back to the

Radius and Arc of the circle. The timeless relationship forever held within the Radius and Arc is the root mathematical formula and visually unfolds to become the first enclosed form of Sacred Geometry, The Circle. The Circle itself is Unity, Oneness and the origin of the "Flower of Life," otherwise known as "Mandala." The Circle is the two-dimensional manifestation of the single point or undivided "God-Mind." The Circle is EVERYTHING- the All. This is the essence of Mandala, verbally expressed as "the Circle holds All."

The Circle is created by rotating the second manifest point of Two (Point B), around the first (Point A). However, the two points are perfect twins with equal potentials. In a Dual system, there can be no discrimination between the one and the other. Point A can therefore, also rotate around Point B, with the creation of an additional circle. This natural polarity, this reversal of roles, produces another circle. These two circles create the first overlapping form of Sacred Geometry, also known as "the Two Circles of Common Radius." These two overlapping circles with common radius create the second enclosed form of Sacred Geometry. The ancients called this archetype, or form, the "Vesica Piscis."

All further forms of this cosmos evolve from the Vesica Piscis. The Vesica Piscis is literally perceived as the womb of the universe. It is the ever-unfolding "Mother" of Sacred Geometry and visually represents the Creative Unity.

.

The Single Point

119

A
•

•
B

Division of the Single Point

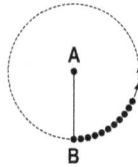

A
•

B

Dual movement establishes the Radius and Arc of the circle

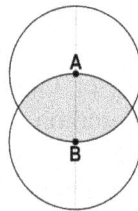

A
•

B

The Circle is created by rotating the second manifest point of Two (Point B), around the first (Point A). Point A can therefore, also rotate around Point B, with the creation of an additional circle.

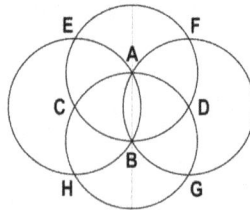

E   F
A
C   D
B
H   G

The Two Circles of Common Radius create two new points at their intersections. The magnification so continues.

In addition to The Vesica Piscis, the Two Circles of Common Radius create two new points at their intersections (points C and D). The play of Father/Mother (points A and B) creates the first children of the universe, also called "the Twins." The magnification so continues.

The Vesica Piscis has been the subject of mystical speculation at several periods of history, perhaps first among the Pythagoreans. The mathematical ratio of its width (measured to the endpoints of the "body," not including the "tail") to its height, was reportedly believed by them to be 265:153 (namely 1.73203...). The geometric ratio of these dimensions represents the square root of 3, or 1.73205 (if straight lines are drawn, connecting the centers of the two circles with each other, with the two points where the circles intersect, two equilateral triangles join along an edge). The ratio 265:153 approximates the square root of three. No better approximation can be obtained by means of any smaller whole number.

"Simon Peter went up and dragged the net to land, full of large fish, one hundred and fifty three; and although there were so many, the net was not broken."

-John 21:11-

Our own relation to this is that it presents itself as a symbol of our creative qualities in the cosmos. More recently, numerous New Age authors have interpreted it as a yonic symbol and claimed that this, as a reference to the female genitals, is a traditional interpretation. *Yoni* is a Sanskrit word that means "womb, vulva, and vagina, place of birth, source, or origin." The word also has a wider meaning in both profane and spiritual contexts, including "spring, fountain, place of rest, repository, receptacle, seat, abode, home, lair, and nest, stable." It is also etymologically derived from the root *yuj*—like *yoga* and *yogini*—meaning, "to join, unite, fasten, or harness." The *yoni* is also considered to be symbolic of Shakti or Devi in Hindu Tantra.

Rotating the first two points (A and B) around the new points (C and D, or the Twins) creates two additional circles and four additional Vesica Piscis. Now we have four circles of common radius and Five Vesica Piscis. The two new circles also create four more points (E, F, G and H) and another enclosed form of Sacred Geometry, known as "The Petal." The Petal is the essence of family, revealed in Sacred Geometry: Parents (circles 1 & 2) and children (circles 3 & 4), with the family heart in the form of a petal. These four circles of common radius is considered to be the germ form of "The Creation Pattern," as all of the necessary forms are now in place. Striking more circles around the new points (E, F, G and H) compounds the forms and creates the possibility of a never-ending grid of Points, Circles, Vesica Piscis, and Petals, entitled Nature's First Pattern.

Nature's First Pattern is the Creation Pattern. All form traces to this pattern. Nature's First Pattern is the ever-evolving two-dimensional pattern, which, at the conceptual level, circumnavigates the universe. There are an infinite number of sub-patterns and -forms to be discovered within Nature's First Pattern, and the study of these unlimited possibilities is proposed as one of the Keys to Sacred Geometry. Sacred Geometry is therefore, presented as the architecture of the Universe and though these symbols we can learn more about the gods and their creative powers. In turn, we learn how to create in the like of the gods.

The Flower of Life, as a product of the Vesica Piscis, is the modern name given to a geometrical figure composed of multiple evenly-spaced, overlapping circles, that are arranged so that they form a flower-like pattern with a six fold symmetry like a hexagon. The center of each circle is on the circumference of six surrounding circles of the same diameter.

The Flower of Life is considered by some to be a symbol of sacred geometry, said to contain ancient, religious value depicting the fundamental forms of space and time. In this sense, it is a visual expression of the connections life weaves through all sentient beings. There are many spiritual beliefs associated with the Flower of Life- for example, depictions of the five Platonic Solids are found within the symbol of Metatron's Cube, which may be derived from the Flower of Life pattern. These platonic solids are geometrical forms, which are said to act as a template from which all life springs. Another notable example of that which may be derived from the Flower of Life is the Tree of Life. This has been an important symbol of sacred geometry for many people from various religious backgrounds. Particularly, the teachings of the Kabala have dealt intricately with the Tree of Life. The Tree of Life is most widely recognized as a mystical concept within the Kabala, which is used to understand the nature of God and the manner in which He created the world ex nihilo (out of nothing). The Cabbalists developed this concept into a full model of reality, using the tree to depict a "map" of creation.

The Flower of Life

The Flower of Life looks like a flower and represents the laws and proportions for everything mortal and immortal; All of Creation.

The Celestial Gods

"how, conformably to what we assert, can the sun and moon, and the visible natures in the heavens, be Gods, if the Gods are alone incorporeal?"

-Porphyry-

"The celestial divinities are not comprehended by bodies, but contain bodies in their divine lives and energies; that they are not themselves converted to body, but they have a body which is converted to its divine cause; and that body does not impede their intellectual and incorporeal perfection, nor occasion them any molestation by its intervention"…." It also imitates a divine life, by the life which is connascent with ethereal bodies."

-Iamblichus-

It is believed that every aspect of the human temperament- from love to bellicosity, from lawfulness to anarchy- had its embodiment within the planets in our solar system. The Pythagoreans called the planets *"cosmocrators,"* or governors of the world. Like the night sky, our psyche is full of mysteries; yet, its darkness and distances too are spotted with patterns, lights, and recognizable figures.[154] We stand between two infinitely vast universes: the macrocosm of the outer world still chary of revealing its many secrets, and the microcosm of the inner world of the psyche, equally possessive of its mysteries.

---

[154] Moore, T. 1989 (Introduction- by Noel Cobb)

Gods and humans cannot be separated. Take the gods away, and dehumanizing sets in. Take away the humans, and the gods lose their power. Any god is limited by the amount of power we allow for it to have. All this is to say that the macrocosm may be allowed some interplay with the microcosm, and that entails a high estimation of human imagination.[155] For a proper understanding of the interplay between the human psyche and the planets, we make use of the work of Marsilio Ficino, an Italian Neoplatonist that lived in the fifteenth century. For Ficino, the external world (macrocosm) is the way to the internal realm of the soul (microcosm). Ficino's Neoplatonism does not advise a retreat from the body. For him, all movement of the soul comes from erōs, which, as previously described, is the factor that knitted the cosmos together in a unified bond. Nature and Man are united in erōs or love. The main point is, however, that the spirit of erōs can break open the psyche; the flame of Erōs, for that is the God we are talking about, sets off an explosion of fantasies and feelings, which may be more significant to the psyche than the relationship.[156] The soul is lured by beauty, for the beauty of the world reflects the beauty of the heavens.

According to Ficino, any image, or perhaps a statue, that represents characteristics of a particular planetary deity, may collect, hold, and bestow the power of that deity on the person by using the image as a medium. Images are awarded deep, archetypal power.[157] In addition, the depth of soul can also be seen in cosmic imagery. We can have depth and variety, movement and form, in our inner world. We can have planets within, with all of their benefits of spirit, like the planets of the outer cosmos.

Since imagination is such an important faculty of the soul, Ficino keeps it in mind even in his "natural magic," which consists

---

[155] Moore, T. 1989 (Introduction- by Noel Cobb)
[156] Moore, T. 1989 (p. 113)
[157] Moore, T. 1989 (p. 38)

chiefly in drawing down the spiritual rays of the planets through visible images or sigils. [158] By keeping in my mind the characters of the planets, knowing especially the spheres of life they "rule," and the images associated with them, we may organize life imaginatively. In *"The Planets"* Ficino remarks, *"Whoever discovers his own genius through the means we have stated will thus find his own natural work, and at the same time he will find his own star and daemon. Following these beginnings, he will do well and live happily. Otherwise, he will experience misfortune and feel the enmity of heaven."*

In general, all gods are jealous. It is warned that each god is ready to assume a monotheistic hold on the individual. This could lead to obsession. In Ficino's psychology, illness comes in the form of monotheism[159], dominated by one single god, with the imagination fixed on one single kind of consciousness. Domination appears as depression, preoccupation with relationship and sexuality, or an abiding and interfering temper of aggressiveness, etc. Ficino's intention is to maintain variety of spirit [polytheism] without getting rid of the dominant one. It is an attempt to find harmony and balance through an imaginative act aimed at making a cosmos of variety and multiplicity in one's psychological environment.[160] The system of Ficino therefore, could be best expressed by using the term "Ecology of the Soul." It is both comprehensive and holistic. The planets lead one toward contemplation and fantasy, having the capacity to entice the soul away from the multiplicity of materialism toward the pleasures of soul-values. When one's psychological life reflects the sky, its planets are in constant motion. It is not stuck under the domination of a single archetype.

The gods are not out in the sky, but neither are they merely poetic terms used to describe personal experiences. In the least, the gods are a psychological reality. A person can therefore,

---

[158] Moore, T. 1989 (p. 53)
[159] Moore, T. 1989 (p. 57)
[160] Moore, T. 1989 (p. 58)

truly take a religious attitude toward the constant flux of motion of the psyche, acknowledging the influence and power of the planets, and drawing their spirit into the fabric of life. As Jung said in his definition of religion, religious sensibility involves giving attention to the contents of psychic life, whether they are known as spirits, gods, daemons, or unconscious fantasies. [161]

The goal of Ficinian theory and practice is a kind of spiritual and psychological harmony: qualities of the soul as well as the body need to be "tempered to a celestial consonance." Appreciation for the images that shape life has an effect on our very sense of self, for one discovers rather quickly, how fluid this "self" is. Tempering affects the person by forcing him or her to make a finer image of him- or herself. Since you understand that nothing is more ordered than heaven and that nothing can be considered more tempered than Jupiter, you may expect that eventually the benefits of the heavens and of Jupiter will follow if you show yourself ordered and tempered in your thoughts, feelings, activities, and way of life. [162] When one imitates Jupiter's characteristics, one's sense of self takes on qualities of that image. Jupiter is that dimension of consciousness through which we find concrete images for our experience without aiming for a single dominant image. Jupiter tempers by constellating all the major processes of the psyche, tuning them to be distinct and effectual. Yet, tuning does not only rule out dissonance- suffering, confusion, enigmas- it actually emphasizes it. Herbs, photography, music, dance, travel, plants, perfumes, artworks of all kinds, museums, airplane rides, novels, meditation, massage, isolation, school, reading, drama, acting, construction, sports, astronomy, and astrology, all of these may be used in tempering the psyche, depending upon the presence of imagination and a genuine concern for soul. Whatever the psyche presents in dream, fantasy, wish, desire,

---

[161] Moore, T. 1989 (p. 198)
[162] Moore, T. 1989 (p. 200)

fear, longing, dread, regret, or love may be imagined and thereby drawn deeper.

The soul can be poorly tempered, and this is a *sickness* of the soul. Monotheism may be considered as a possible cause of *sickness* of the soul. Alcmaeon of Croton, a Pythagorean physician of 500 BCE, held that "equality of rights between qualities of moist, dry, cold, hot, bitter, sweet, and the rest, preserved health, but the rule of one among them [*monarchia*] produced sickness." One advantage among many of the polytheistic psyche is the variety of psychological experience it allows. A tempered polytheistic psyche, containing all the planets and their rays/ spirits, enjoys a variety of powers otherwise excluded by a monarchial consciousness or simply by lack of imaginative depth.

- **Sol**

The sun is important for maintaining life. It is visible in its brilliance, influential in its warmth, and so obvious as to be taken for granted. Worldwide, devoted worship of the sun attests to its spiritual significance. The sun represents spirit itself. [163]

Ficino develops this idea further in *The Planets*:

---

[163] Moore, T. 1989 (p. 127)

"Similarly, the World Soul flourishes everywhere, but especially through the sun, as it indiscriminately unfolds its common power of life"

Everything is contained within the Sun, as the Monad or Irreducible Unity of this System. It is the center of the planetary system, as an ever-present quality! Sol is the Light of consciousness, shed on the dark mysteries of nature, so that an increase of solar influence corresponds to a heightening of consciousness. It therefore, depicts the "Higher Self."

Together with earth, the sun represents a union between body and soul. Psychologically, the individual neither flees contact with body and feminine reality, nor does he immerse himself in the material world to the neglect of spirit. Psyche needs the sexual touch of spirit and matter if it is so to be fed, fertilized, and embodied. To be too much in the sun is to have an overdose of spirit.

The night of spirit, the sinking of consciousness, the "dark night of the soul," is a necessary movement in the natural rhythm of light and darkness. [164]

Sources of solar spirit: gold, moss, nutmeg, amber, honey, myrrh, incense, cinnamon, aloes, and other aromatic materials, etc.

---

[164] Moore, T. 1989 (p. 36)

- **Venus**

When Ficino explains how to make an archetypal model of the universe, he declares, "Naturally it should be completed under the guidance of the goddess of beauty." Venus circumvents the ravaging spirit of Saturn. As the goddess of love, she represents both human and divine love. The mythological Venus is the daughter of Uranus, the sky. She is immaterial, having no father or mother, nor the limitations of matter. She lives between the Cosmic Mind and the sub-lunar world. She, as ruler over the season spring, presides over the fertility of the earth. Yet, she is also the goddess advocating movement away from earth (the physical realm) towards heaven (the spiritual realm). Full, sensuous involvement in the beauty of body and nature "arouses one to move to higher regions of spirit, but both are necessary."[165]

Venus is moist in herself, saturated with emotion and sensation. Venus's Gift then, is spirit, but it is a peculiar kind of spirituality, one quite sensual. There is spirit to be gained from her sensuality, sexuality, and absorption in pleasure, and therefore her domain is pleasant for soul. Obviously, Venus can entice the soul toward full absorption into sensuality. [166]

Ficino notes there is an opposition between Venus and Sol: if we devote ourselves properly to Venus, we will not easily enjoy

---

[165] Moore, T. 1989 (p. 141)
[166] Moore, T. 1989 (p. 144)

130

the sun. However, if we are properly concerned with Sol, we will also not enjoy Venus. More specifically, it seems as if Venus's moisture is incompatible with the drying effect of solar consciousness. Yet, the soul must host both planets regularly.[167] Psyche needs dryness as well as moisture!

Venus grants proper spirit to one's overall psychological condition: her psychic body, sensation, aesthetic sense, growth, pleasure, and concrete understanding.

Venus transcends human limits, insofar as she is the goddess of the generation and growth of all life. Her negative qualities manifest indecency, shame, and dark secrecy. Yet, our current compulsive fascination with Venus stems from our long neglect of her, perhaps because of our prudishness and her indecency. If that is the case, we might imagine a possible world climate, which gives the goddess her due. [168]

- **Mercury**

Mercury is most often depicted as bright, quick and light. Mercury can lift soul out of the limitations of a materialistic view of things. For Renaissance polytheists, Mercury is closely related to the Egyptian Thoth (the Greek Hermes), god of secret

---

[167] Moore, T. 1989 (p. 144)
[168] Moore, T. 1989 (p. 146)

Wisdom, and to the Babylonian Nebo, god of writing. Writing and speaking with clarity and wit was regarded as a Mercurial gift. It is no secret that Mercury is concerned not only with the communication of words but also with the interpretation of the speaker's mind. Interpretation- hermeneutics- is of the essence of the Mercurial spirit. [169]

Mercury excites memory. The virtues associated with mercury include eloquence, versatility, wit, acuteness, genius, artfulness, imagination, and cleverness. Mercury reveals an inner realm of things without depriving them of their concreteness. Mercury has the power to put souls to sleep or waken them with his staff. Mercurial consciousness wakens the souls. The advantage of Mercurial intelligence is its power to keep the soul in motion, spiraling down toward a vortex of significance. [170]

Mercurial consciousness "thieves" ideas and suggestions from two places- from other people (such as during a conversation) and from the complexes and archetypes of the psyche itself. As Hermes, Mercury also guides souls to the underworld. Mercury awakens psychological consciousness by discovering within ourselves that structure of consciousness by which we see the many dimensions of significance that dwell in and through the literal. Mercury makes us aware of those aspects that translate into psychological consciousness.

Sol provides the necessary spirit and Venus the required sensual experience, while Mercury provides the channel for Apollonian light, allowing us to bring the psychological stratum of meaning into our purview. [171] It provides the link between understanding why two opposing forces exist.

---

[169] Moore, T. 1989 (p. 149)
[170] Moore, T. 1989 (p. 153)
[171] Moore, T. 1989 (p. 155)

- **Luna**

Luna is the moistest of planets, implying that she is nearest to Earth. Luna is in touch with experience, saturated with the feelings of the concrete, and participant in other functions of moisture in nature and in the soul. Lunar qualities are more crude and moist than the subtle and volatile nature of spirit. Luna has much to do with the human body and the processes of nature. Luna is the gateway to embodiment and personalization of fantasies, complexes, and archetypal possibilities. She stands, true to her typical soul image, as a bridge between the personal and the archetypal. Luna within is sensed as the consciousness of supra-personal or unconscious realities which play a role in life, but are not conscious creations. [172]

Lunar consciousness appears personal. Lunar activity by which collective fantasies are made personal is a downward movement, a tendency toward the concrete and individual. Lunar watchfulness ensures good timing, and a full awareness of body and soul, their individual movements and their motion in relation to each other. For both soul and nature, Luna is a guide to favorable rhythms and seasons.

Of all the planets, Luna moves the fastest. Lunar consciousness implies an awareness of the time zones of body and soul. To get these zones synchronized is a major goal with lunar

---

[172] Moore, T. 1989 (p. 156-7)

consciousness. Much of the pain of living comes from a lack of coordination between the body and soul. [173]

The moon does indeed reflect in her striking and obvious transformations the progress of a personal lifetime: human life itself exhibits this lunar character. It suggests the dynamics of episodes in the personal life- the waxing and waning, the fullness and emptiness, the beginnings and endings, which shape and tone the ways in which we embody the movements of soul. Becoming involved more intimately with the processes of psyche entails familiarity with these lunar phases.

Connected with the rhythms of Luna is the obvious fact that Luna's light is a mere reflection of the light of the sun. Lunar consciousness is by nature reflective, leaving the initiative to Sol, in whom all the planetary spirits are united. Though always in motion, Luna's function is to receive the light of Sol, therefore she is also rather passive. The way back to the light and to psychological awareness is through these reflections, tracing them back to their origins, in the same manner, as we would trace back qualities of the Monad, via the lower emanations. In Lunar consciousness personal life is emptied as well as filled, a round that has as much darkness as light. Death is always close to creativity. Expect movements of decay as well as growth and do not interpret them as inappropriate. Waning or waxing, full moon or sliver-crescent may be sensed at any time with reference to one of the many motions of the psyche. The Moon, it is said, is the conveyor of the virtue of all the planets.

---

[173] Moore, T. 1989 (p. 159)

- **Saturn**

It is only Mars and Saturn that present possible danger to the soul. Within Saturn, heaviness laid the treasures of deep religious contemplation and artistic genius. Saturn is the god of Roman religion and mythology. Among the children of the hoary god are geometers, carpenters, latrine cleaners, and grave digger- all occupations we will see indicating a facet of Saturn's spiritual influence.

In Greek mythology, the god Kronos (Chronos) represents Saturn. Kronos, was the leader and the youngest of the first generation of Titans, divine descendants of Gaia, the earth, and Uranus, the sky. He overthrew his father and ruled during the mythological Golden Age, until he was overthrown by his own sons, Zeus, Hades, and Poseidon, and imprisoned in Tartarus or sent to rule the paradise of the Elysian Fields. Because of his association with the virtuous Golden Age, Kronos was worshipped as a harvest deity, overseeing crops such as grains, nature and in general, agriculture. He was usually depicted with a sickle, which he used to harvest crops and which was also the weapon he used to castrate his father. Kronos' father, Uranus, had many children by his female partner, Gaia, but Uranus hid them from Gaia. Gaia, as might be expected, mourned for her lost children, but she also sought revenge. As it turned out, Kronos was the only one of her children willing to risk everything in going up against Uranus. Aided with a *sickle*, supplied by Gaia, Kronos was able to castrate Uranus -- an act generally interpreted as an event separating heaven from earth.

We must at all costs avoid his harmful influence and especially his power to desiccate the soul; on the other hand, it is only by going through Saturn, experiencing his spirit to the hilt, which we can gain the positive benefit he has to offer. Just as within the story of Kronos we find the young man who dares to create a space between sky and earth, opening up a middle realm where perhaps the soul can exist, so in other stories and images of Saturn we find a shining reward within the darkness of his malevolence. The phase of malevolence represents psychologically that phase of the soul's work when the mess that has been made, is allowed to settle, rot and putrefy. Death and darkness penetrate the realm of Saturn, and as Ficino warns, either blackness will attract the influence of Saturn, or Saturn will bring with him feelings of death and decay. [174]

Saturn does not easily symbolize a quality and power common to the human race, but a person cut off from others- divine or bestial, blessed or overwhelmed with extreme misfortune. In the story of Kronos, his final fate is to rule at the end of the world, far from the activities of ordinary life.

During depression, deep within, it would seem that something is going on and attention is being taken from the outside world and applied elsewhere. Saturn lives on old and outdated fantasies, which, since they have no inherent signs of vitality, he must bolster, patch and defend. Saturnian souls are quite involved in construction: building, ordering, collecting, analyzing and planning.

Deprived of the moisture of fresh fantasy, we are forced to build worlds out of old and dry ideas, giving a definite Saturnian flavor to much of our culture. The stone buildings, geometrical forms, and styles from an idealized past, features found on

---

[174] Moore, T. 1989 (p. 167)

many campuses and government complexes, betray signs of Saturn's rule.

Being in Saturn, we have lost touch with the movement of soul: the planets, lunar reality, and the surface of earth. We are far away within, in Saturn, the most remote of the planets and the coldest. We have not lost something so much as we ourselves are lost at the rim of our inner zodiac, at the end of the world. Saturn is indeed the god of a closing time. He wants full control over the past and the future, and his first and often repeated words- "it is finished"- identify him with a dying god, an eternal moment of death. [175] Therefore, in Saturn, there is no ending point, no conclusion, only a frozen, dried-out state of death.

Saturn is to be avoided when his spirit would dry out the soul and adversely affect the body. Yet, in Saturn, we can find a degree of contemplation equal to the severity of his wickedness. Ficino advises us to get deep into our depression and stay with them long enough to allow their work to have an effect. Feeling low and heavy we are forced to move inward, turning to fantasy rather than the literal action of the ego. In addition, that inward turn is necessary for the soul, for it creates psychic space, a container for deeper reflection where soul increases and the surface of events becomes less important. [176]

Saturn pushes us to the edge where our imagery becomes primordial, refined, and removed from our usual patterns of reflection, our accustomed imagery, and personal reference. Instead of earthly life from which Saturn himself is removed, he confers celestial and eternal life on you. The reward to be found in feelings of melancholy, depression and heaviness stems directly from the withdrawal from life those feelings encourage. Saturn is therefore, not simply a troublesome planet to be avoided- with perseverance and endurance, we may find in his dark, heavy, ambivalent moods a way through and beyond the shallowness of the present.

---

[175] Moore, T. 1989 (p. 170)
[176] Moore, T. 1989 (p. 171)

- **Jupiter**

♃

Jupiter represents the god of the common life, the deity who represents, above all, those things, which keep life moderate, especially laws and government, the maintenance of social and civic life. Jupiter is intellect from which the universe is produced. He may be imaged as man, since essentially man is mind.[177]

Life can become routine and unconsciously stuck in materialistic projects; it degenerates because it has been cut off from its generative fantasies. However, life can be revived and ensouled again, through the skilful use of images. Reflecting on Jupiter we re-create soul and nourish it through the spirit contained in material forms- or the images that permeate life. Society is not only a collection of people, it is also a theater of images. When we put up buildings or establish a social agency, we are also creating an image. Jupiter makes us aware of the things of this world, so obvious and overlooked, that serve as "magic decoys" that can lure us back to a psychological perspective and once again put us in touch with our fantasies. Jupiter gives back soul to society.

Jupiter's role is to provide the specific intelligence needed to build a culture and to keep it vital. He is that form of imagination by which we transform our visions into realities of

---

[177] Moore, T. 1989 (p. 174)

collective living. Culture is a source of spirit and the imaginative creation of fantasy.

The liberal disciplines- art, grammar, poetry, oratory, rhetoric, painting, sculpture, architecture, and music, belong to Jupiter. Jupiter is the source of the most humanly significant spirit. Along with Mercury and Sol, he is among the human of the planets.[178] Jupiter is that spirit most important to human life because it both shares in the spirit of other nourishing planets and moderates them for human tolerance. Jupiter serves as an indirect path to spirit. He remains close to the flow of life, the excitement and traumas of social involvement, and the mundane, concrete details of fabricating and fashioning culture.

Jupiter aims at fulfilling the two extremes of human concern- spirit and body- and it gathers them at a midpoint that is psychological. [179]

- **Mars**

Mars remains for the most part a detrimental factor in the life of the psyche, to be avoided or at least mollified. Mars represents anger, violence, war, hatred, bitterness, and also heroism. One can go find the benefit of Mars only after facing the full potential of his detrimental side.

---

[178] Moore, T. 1989 (p. 177)
[179] Moore, T. 1989 (p. 180)

Mars keeps a stronghold on humanity. War and violence are still so widespread and are pursued with such self-righteous spirit as to threaten our very existence daily.[180] One comes across so many instances where an individual is "at war with himself." Beneath and beyond these personal factors there is the archetypal, essentially human and trans-human force of conflict, battle and rage- Mars himself! Martian things are like poison, as a natural enemy to spirit. We may tend to keep Martian spirit out of our "temperament," because we find it morally toxic; yet, perhaps by keeping anger outside the realm of moral possibility, we allow for incursions of more violent forms of Martian spirit.

Mars warms the coldest things and energizes the sluggish. Venus (Aphrodite) tames Mars, yet, she does not interfere with the nobility he provides. Aphrodite's love can obviously wield immense power, charming our senses and souls, but she need not root out our nobility, the presence of Mars. Mars can intensify love and embolden the lover. Yet, in spite of this, Mars is still poison.

Mars, in his fiery realism counters sentimental ideals of integration and wholeness, and he allows the psyche to exist in the brilliance of its many centers. The planets themselves are multiple, reflective of the many facets of the psyche which resist harmonization. Mars plays an important role in establishing that harmony and in creating the nobility of spirit equal to a polytheistic psyche. We can therefore, not deny Mars a role in the orchestra of the psyche.

---

[180] Moore, T. 1989 (p. 184)

Practice

The magician needs to create a mandala/sigil from the Flower of Life. The word "Mandala," is rooted in Sanskrit and literally means "Circle," which is the first enclosed archetype of Sacred Geometry. The contemplation of Sacred Geometry through the processes of studying or creating a Flower of Life (open-eyed meditation) brings the individual in close communion with the gods. For the soul's to return to the divine demands that it ritually reenact cosmogenesis. When the soul activates the power of the appropriate symbols, the presence of the gods in the soul is awakened. The Flower of Life in this regard acts as a metaphysical doorway to the gods, because it contains "All" from which "all" were created. It therefore, represents every component of cosmogenesis as a mathematical symbol thereof. In this respect, it is important to remember that all matter (the four elements) was believed to be composed of the symmetrical solids- earth was cubical, fire tetrahedral, water icosahedral and air, octahedral and the magician could, in addition, apply them into his/ her own practice. One can find within the Flower of Life all the building blocks of the universe that are reasoned to represent the Platonic Solids.

The Flower of Life can be used as a metaphor to illustrate the connectedness of man and the gods, within the universe. The Platonic Solids are considered as important because they are found in the rudimentary construction of organic life, as well as music, language, and consciousness itself. The Flower of Life shows how the Platonic Solids serve as templates through which the foundation of all life everywhere can be expressed. From the models within it, the Flower of Life symbol has the ability to demonstrate how all things come from one source and are intimately and permanently woven together.

The individual can apply different techniques towards achieving union with the creative gods that reside in the magician, with the Flower of Life as a basis. It is possible to prepare a Mandala from paper, in any size, or even reflect the Flower of Life against a wall, as a means of meditation. It can serve as an additional adornment on the Altar (together with your usual symbols). What is important is that the individual meditate on the symbol and what it represents, which is "Everything."

A more elaborate use would be for the magician to perform a rite in which the Flower of Life symbol is prepared on the surface of the earth and accented by references to the Four Cardinal Directions. Each of the four quadrants is marked in colors symbolizing the powers of the four directions and the natural seasons:

- South (Yellow): representing the Sun, the source of all life. The South is the place of the child;
- West (Blue): representing the mysterious, transcendental powers of darkness. The West brings internal illumination;
- North (Black and White): representing test, trial, and survival. The North brings wisdom;
- East (Red): representing renewal. The East is associated with awakening. The East represents Daytime and illumination;
- The additional directions: Below (Mother/ Earth), Above (Father/ Sky) and Center (Man).

It is important here to acknowledge the role of the circle. It is not a circle of protection but rather represents the Ouroboros (also spelled Oroborus, Uroboros or Uroborus), an ancient symbol depicting a snake or dragon swallowing its tail, constantly creating itself and forming a circle. If indeed the magician would like to include a protective circle, an additional circle should be drawn outside that of the outer border of the Flower of Life.

It is advisable that the ritual be performed under the open sky, with appropriate incense and other paraphernalia. Approach the ritual as you would any other. You may add some dramatic elements, such as the use of stage make-up or appropriate music*. The magician should also have a chalice filled with wine# and placed on the altar. The wine corresponds to earth; the

---

*Music: Music is like air, and is carried on and through the air to the ear, where it has easy access to the spirit of the listener. Music is a product of mind, imagination and feeling, and therefore it readily stimulates the same faculties in the listener. In a sense, music is a quality of the soul itself, an elemental factor in its constitution, parallel to the air element in nature. One is in the music, not outside of it. Ficino compares the element of air, with that of the Greek god Apollo. Apollo's music is by nature subtle and spiritual, but it is nevertheless exciting and moving and offers all the psychological advantages necessary. Ficino reasons that if we have a sky within and planets making their "music of the spheres" in our very soul, then music is to be found in the rhythms of these planets. "As above, so below," the alchemists were fond of saying. As the planets of the soul enter and fade and play through the psyche in varying counterpoints, their movements, felt in emotion and fantasy, give musical form to the very structures of our consciousness. Aristotle himself believed that *"Rhythms and melodies contain representations of anger and mildness, and also of courage and temperance and all their opposites and the other moral qualities, that most closely correspond to the true natures of these qualities (and this is clear from the facts of what occurs- when we listen to such representations we change in our soul)."* Cassiodorus speaks of these virtues and moral qualities as musical in themselves, making the psyche itself musical. For him, music of the soul consists in the harmony of good habits and virtues- a virtuous life is a musical life. Ficino conceives human music as the proper arrangement of one's life so that all concrete experiences resonate, like overtones, the fundamental octave of possibilities represented by the planet-tones. Psychotherapy would be musical then insofar as one would temper and tune the planetary tonal centers so that each would hum within the surface events of life.

#Wine: The wine represents our "thirst" for spiritual vitality, the resistance of ego, manifest in all accomplishments and failures of the past. The wine represents the gods Bacchus or Greek Dionysus, the god of wine, among other things. Dionysus is the dying and rising god, a reflection of the Egyptian Osiris, worshipped as the god of the

aroma of wine takes the place of water; the songs and musical melodies represent air. A black candle[#] should be placed on the altar (in addition to the candles you use as part of your rituals). The candle represents the element of fire.

Stand in the center of the Flower of Life. Repeat nine times:

"Zazas zazas nassatanada zazas"

---

underworld. Osiris represents dismemberment. To experience the Dionysian affirmation of life, one has to be torn apart. The tight hold of the ego loosens. Wine, corresponding to the element earth, is the psyche's body and represents things physical and sensual- body experienced psychologically. [181] Dionysus is a stirring of the soul and body, an eruption of life from its vibrant source, a simultaneous brush with the terrors and ecstasies of life and death. It has the capacity to bring pleasure. Ficino's second element of the psyche parallels water, and it too represents the process of dissolution. The aroma of the wine stands in relation to wine itself, as water to earth. Here, Dionysian dismemberment through sensuality, pleasure and drunken madness (the dissolution of reason) appears more complete, and consciousness has been rendered psychological. The aroma of wine is more suited to the nature of soul itself, invisible, but perceptible and efficacious. Neglected values, unfinished situations, and forgotten ideals return to inebriate the soberness of the present. These stories and images of the past have an aroma, a spirit and tone, which can nourish the soul. They are fragrances of the psyche.

[#]**The Black Candle/ Light**: Through participation in light, we have knowledge of the things of our world and of ourselves, because light is knowledge. We talk of "en**light**enment." This is the crowning of psyche and its prime spiritual nourishment. It is not the product of human ratiocination but rather the gift of the God Apollo, the sun god. He offers us entry into an image of brilliance, a fantasy of light. The light produced by a simple candle fire reflects in a simple way the fire of the stars; our individual ideas and wishes can be traced back to large movements of the soul, to multiply structures of consciousness and habits of thinking represented by the many planets "burning" in the night sky. Light is intelligence, a kind of knowing. The goal is to

---

[181] Moore, T. 1989 (p. 81)

Light the black candle, then say:

"I now participate in the light of reason"

Followed by:

"I summon the Lord of all Creation. Ageless Intelligence of the Cosmos, who roams this world. Be with me now. For I am as you are. Come forth. For one who is of your essence seeks your presence."

Before drinking from the grail, say:

"Vita vinum est!" (Life is wine)

"In vino veritas" (The wisdom is in the wine)

Now summon the elements:

"The Four Unite into One
When Darkness unfolds the arms
And the Serpent takes hold
Awaken to Night
Rise up as the Source of Intelligence"

Invocation of the planets:

"I am the Master of Form, and from me all forms proceed"

Sol
Sol Sol Sol
Sal-sel-sil-sol-sul
a-e-i-o-u
SSSSSOOOOOl Sol Sol
Venus
Venus Venus Venus
va-ve-vi-vo-vu
un-an-in-en-on
VEEEEEENNNIIISSS

---

develop an Apollonian, lucid insight into the deep patterns at work in ordinary experience.

Mercury
Mercury Mercury Mercury
ka-ke-ki-ko-ku
ra-re-ri-ro-ru
MMMERCCCUUURRREEE
Luna
Luna Luna Luna
lu-la-li-le-lo
nu-na-ni-ne-no
LLUUUNNNAAA
Saturn
Saturn Saturn Saturn
sa-se-si-so-su
tu-ta-ti-te-to
SSSAATTTUUUNN
Jupiter
Jupiter Jupiter Jupiter
Ja-ju-jo-je-ji
pa-pe-pi-po-pu
JJJUUUPPPTTTRRR
Mars
Mars Mars Mars
ma-me-mi-mo-mu
su-so-si-se-sa
MMMRRRSSS

"I am that pure magician who is in the mouth and body of the
universal architect
Behold, for I am in everything
At the stroke of a word, I invest my power in the vital essence of
any element
My powers put fear into the gods who come into being after me
I am the One who made heaven and established it
I shall be with it for eternity which time begets"

Extinguish the Black Candle

Close the Gate and finish with the words, *"So Mote it Be!"*

*"Pythagoras holds that number moves itself, and he takes
number as an equivalent for intelligence."*

Background

To pursue the division of sunthēmata into material,
intermediate and noetic categories, the soul's noetic powers
would have to be transformed by noetic objects, and that these
would be best exemplified in numbers. An implicit arithmetic
influence is evident already in the intermediate sunthēmata. If
mathematic elements functioned for Iamblichus as sunthēmata
it was because of their "horizontal" expression as rational
formulas. Their intelligibility alone did not make them Theurgic,
but their capacity to create noetic rhythms capable of receiving
the gods. Here they must be understood as ritual objects and
that one may worship the gods through them. Mathematic
elements are fully evident in the Tiamaeus where the Demiurge
creates the World-Soul out of geometric, harmonic and
arithmetic proportions. [182]

In *De Anima* Iamblichus reviews the soul as a mathematical
essence. He lists three positions:

1) Soul as geometrical figure;
2) Soul as number, and
3) Soul as harmony.

It is clear that Platonic and Pythagorean philosophers identified
the soul with different branches of the mathematical. On
account of this, then, the soul coexists together with the
geometric, arithmetic and harmonic proportions, so that by

---

[182] Shaw, G. 1951. (p. 191)

analog the soul is identical with [all] mathematical ratios. [183] The variety and vitality of nature was simply concrete manifestations of numerical powers. This relationship is recognized by a number of historical and contemporary magicians.

In strictly Platonic terms, the soul was a mathematical entity. For Pythagoreans the study of numbers therefore, was a religious experience. They considered mathematics to reveal divine mysteries. The soul's mental projection of mathematic images initiated a ritual activity that affected the soul's return to its true self. Just as the material powers of the soul were divinized through material sacrifices, and the intermediate powers were divinized by visual or audible images, so the noetic powers of the soul were divinized through the mental imagery of mathematic objects. [184] By means of it the soul was able to bring the mind into resonance with the numbers of the World-Soul. Iamblichus says the mathematical mysteries of the Pythagoreans purified the mind and allowed it to participate in the gods. Each god was associated with a geometric figure that appeared in the heavens at critical moments and that these figures were employed at such times in some form of Theurgic worship. [185]

Based on the evidence, however, it may be inferred that the geometric figures of the gods functioned as contemplative icons, perhaps like the geometric mandalas of yogic disciplines. The mandala is at once a manifestation of the divinity. However, the mandala also serves as a receptacle for the gods.

Although Iamblichus denied that the discursive use of numbers was Theurgic, he knew that as a numerical entity the soul eventually had to undergo a numerical transformation. Just as material souls were united with material gods through material sunthēmata, noetic souls were united with the immaterial Nous

---

[183] Shaw, G. 1951. (p. 193)
[184] Shaw, G. 1951. (p. 195)
[185] Shaw, G. 1951. (p. 202)

through mathematical sunthēmata. This form of Theurgy might initially have been a discursive exercise: mathematics visualizations, but at a certain point, the visualizations would spontaneously become visions empowered by the gods. The "noetic Theurgist" is "above all law" because he was above its effects, having become the living embodiment of the gods. After all, since the laws of ritual reflected the order of the gods, a divinized soul would have been assimilated to that order and hence to the laws of hieratic worship. He was no longer under the law, because he *was* the law. [186]

The Age of Satan (Set-HerWar) and "The Ceremony of the Nine Angles"

Late 1972 Anton Szandor LaVey's third book "The Satanic Rituals – Companion to the Satanic Bible" appeared in the bookstores. This book contained a collection of rituals and ceremonies some of which are not originally by LaVey. LaVey distinguishes between ritual and ceremony based on the inherent ability of a ritual to affect its practitioner, whereas as ceremony, on the other hand, is merely a pageant or a play for psychodramatic illustration of a favored belief or philosophy.[187] Aquino highlights that there is a fine line between rituals and ceremonies, as a moving ceremony will tend to influence individuals ritualistically.

One of these rituals "The Ceremony of the Nine Angles," was the first true LHP rite based on the Pythagorean Number System, published publicly. In fact, LaVey himself was not the mastermind behind this magical working, but rather Dr. Michael Aquino, a then member of the Priesthood of the Church of Satan, who wrote the Ceremony of the Nine Angles as part of his thesis towards the level of Magister Caverni of the VI°.

---

[186] Shaw, G. 1951. (p. 209)
[187] Aquino, M. 2009. (p. 237)

Even though the Ceremony of the Nine Angles was written within the context of the Age of Satan, it is still considered a powerful and valid tool within the constructs of current LHP traditions. In the Ceremony of the Nine Angles, Dr. Aquino applied the system of Iamblichus as a method of Black Magic. The System fitted perfectly into the trapezoidal Seal, which was also the symbol used to identify the Priesthood of the original Church of Satan, containing the trihedral angles as a truncated pyramid, with the power of the trapezoid perfectly manifest, in a golden Section-based three-dimensional structure.

Setian Cosmology

It is important to remember that the true LHP Initiate is free to create his own "religion" or to accept or reject elements of preexisting systems according to his needs or Will. Yet, for the sake of understanding the conceptual framework of the Ceremony of the Nine Angles, it is important to have a basic understanding of Setian cosmology.

The core of Dr. Aquino's (the author of the Ceremony of the Nine Angles and founder of the Temple of Set) cosmology is solidly Platonic.[188] He has become a modern exemplary model for a Lord of the Transcendental Brach of the LHP. Individual Setian thought begins with the logical suppositions and proceeds from them to more magical conclusions based on experience. The Setian cosmology is posited as the best possible answer to fundamental philosophical and magical questions given the data available- it remains, however, open to evolution should any fallacy be identified or further data become known.[189] Setian philosophy follows the reasoning that what can be explained by assuming fewer things should not be explained by assuming more.

---

[188] Flowers, S.E. 1997. (p. 216)
[189] Flowers, S.E. 1997. (p. 229)

The first assumption is that there exists a Universe defined as the "totality of existence both known and unknown by humanity." Within this internally consistent framework exists the Objective Universe, which is explained as "the vast expanses of space and the masses of animate and inanimate matter and energy occupying it." Beyond this, there exists the subjective universe- the psyche distinguished from the objective universe- that is both apprehensive and creative.[190] The clearest, simplest, and yet most profound symbol of the Setian cosmology is provided by the Pentagram of Set. The perfect circle around the pentagram represents the "mathematical order of the objective universe." The pentagram does not touch the circle "signifying that the Powers of Darkness are not derived from or dependent upon" the natural order. Basic Setian cosmology therefore, provides a theoretical framework sufficient for the basic and essential Black Magical initiatory work.

In the Setian universe, Set, just as other archetypes in the Left-Hand Path, can be approached theistically or non-theistically. Set represents pure Intelligence. Set Himself developed an understanding of His Intelligence by using Pythagorean "creative principles" as described in *From the abstract to the concrete.*" In the *Book of Coming Forth by Night*, Set states:

> "*I am the ageless Intelligence of this Universe. I created HarWer [Horus] that I might define my Self. All other gods of all other time and nations have been created by men. This you know…. From my manifest semblance, which alone is not of Earth.*"

Set is therefore, Intelligence, defined, made finite and given shape, by the Objective Universe (HarWer) which it created to provide that shape and definition. By itself, Set learns his own qualities based on creation of a dual system, in which HarWer serves as the one anti-pole. This conflicted nature makes HarWer the "Opposite Self of Set." The "separation process" between Set and HarWer is the theological or cosmological equivalent of the rebellion of the angels in heaven in the Judeo-

---

[190] Flowers, S.E. 1997. (p. 230)

Christian system. The implications are, of course, also quite different. In the Setian view the "conflict" is implicit and a matter of essence, not explicit and a matter or "morality."[191]

In this cosmology, there is an inherent "dualism" between nature and "non-nature" which echoes the ancient Greek distinction between nature and psyche (intellect). This distinction is also projected into the Universe as a whole, positing that the Objective Universe and the Subjective Universe exist in reality.[192]

"Intellect, therefore, which is the leader and king of all beings, and which is the demiurgic art of the universe, is always present with the Gods with invariable sameness."

-Iamblichus-

The human being is seen as possessing a non-natural component, the psyche (or intellect), which is logically of non-natural origin. This non-natural component is referred to as "the Gift of Set" (previously identified as the Gift of Satan/ Lucifer). Setian philosophy is therefore, a psychecentric one- that is, it focuses the attention of the subject of any act of Will back upon the subject or one doing the action. The structure of this subject is called the psyche, soul, intellect, ba (in Egyptian), and so on. Set is the general Principle, the individual psyche of a Setian is the specific manifestation.

---

[191] Flowers, S.E. 1997. (p. 232)
[192] Flowers, S.E. 1997. (p. 230)

"I am the Magus of the Word Xeper (pronounced Khefer), an English language coinage expressing an Egyptian verb written as a stylized scarab and meaning "I Have Come Into Being." This Word generates the Aeon of Set, and is the current form of the Eternal Word of the Prince of Darkness. To Know this Word is to know that the ultimate responsibility for the evolution of your psyche is in your hands. It is the Word of freedom, ecstasy, fearful responsibility, and the root of all Magic." [193]

-Don Webb-

[193] http://www.xeper.org/pub/lib/lib_xeper.htm

The Law of the Trapezoid

"We all react to what we see. Just as sounds and odors influence our behavior, so do visual patterns and shapes. Fear is the prime mover. Any shape or spatial concept that triggers fear could therefore be considered "evil." The most disturbing shape of all is a trapezoid in its myriad forms. A perfect trapezoid is a frustrated pyramid. In fact, the place where a pyramid or triangle is lopped off to make a trapezoid is called a "frustum." Angles are space-planes that provoke anxiety- that is, those not harmonious with natural visual orientation- will engender aberrant behavior."[194]

When applied correctly, these Laws can be used to the benefit of Self-change. It is important to state that inclusion of the Law is not based on its ability to "daemonize" social behavior, but rather due to its impact on the individual psyche to cause Self-change. Angles (figures or spaces made up of obtuse or acute angles) are space-planes that provoke foremost visceral anxiety or fear (unless they are recognized as such)- even if unconscious- which could serve as a catalyst for self-transformation. In this sense, fear is considered as a shadow.

"Angles" form an abstract construct, which gives shape to LaVey's cosmology. "The Law of the Trapezoid" most precisely describes these "angles," or geometrical models that seem to have power to create certain effects in the objective and subjective universes. LaVey makes his most magically potent statement on the power of the Angles in the ritual text of *Die elektrischen Vorspiele* first published in the Satanic Rituals (p. 106-30). LaVey speaks of a Barrier outside of which are predatory beasts (Hounds) which can enter and exit this world through "angles" according to certain "cycles." The basic idea for this ritual came from *"The Hounds of Tindalos"* by F.B. Long,

---

[194] LaVey, A.S. 1992. (p. 111-116)

who is one of the Lovecraft circle.[195] LaVey considered attraction as a major component of the Nine Angles. He described this attractive property of angles as "The Command to Look," based on the title of a photography book in which some common angular properties of certain attractive images were discussed.

The "Ceremony of the Nine Angles" was not meant to change the outside world so much as it was designed to alter the feelings and attitudes of those participating in the ritual- to free them of detrimental emotions (fear, guilt, etc.) or to give expression to forbidden desires, feelings, or thoughts. The Satanic Rituals is a collection of this type of psycho dramatic ceremonies.

It is important here to acknowledge that the "Ceremony of the Nine Angles" goes well beyond the Law of the Trapezoid. The magic connected with the Trapezoid has a unique character, unlike any other school of magic. In theory, Trapezoidal magic makes use of geometrical manipulations of the ritual environment (visual and spatial), the creation of certain electromagnetic fields in the chamber (ionization etc.) and the manipulation of light and sound waves to establish ideal psycho physiological conditions for the focus, concentration and projection of the Will of the magician to any part of the universe. To do this, technical apparatus such as Tesla coils, Van de Graaf generators, strobe lights, etc. are used in a ritual context, which is published in Die elektrischen Vorspiele, also in The Satanic Rituals. The magician is reminded that this equipment can be physically harmful and no attempt should be made to apply them, unless the magician has sufficient background to do so. At present, such magical explorations are an ongoing concern and area of expertise in the Order of the Trapezoid, within the Temple of Set. [196; 197]

---

[195] Flowers, S.E. 1997 (p. 191)
[196] Flowers, S.E. 1997. (p. 207)
[197] http://www.trapezoid.org/

Today, a number of LHP occult groups and orders effectively apply the Nine Angles as method of magic. One such Order, the Order of the Trapezoid, is the oldest, largest and most active and diverse Orders in the Temple of Set. Other groups, such as the ONA, Order of the Nine Angles, also use derivatives of the Nine Angles as insignia, even though the author of this text has limited knowledge as to the degree to which the angles themselves play a central role in their practice of magic.

The Seal of Runa

The Seal of Runa

The Seal of Runa is the personal seal of Dr. Stephen Edred Flowers. It contains the Trapezoidal Seal, with additions that render a more holistic representation of the Trapezoid. The word *"Runa"* is a translation of the word *"Mystery,"* but it is advised that the reader seek additional sources to clarify this concept, as it is not within the scope of this treatise to deal with it.

The Nine Angles (the pentagram fitted inside a trapezoid) is symbolically presented as encircled by the Circle of Life, or Ouroboras. The Ouroboros is an ancient symbol depicting a serpent or dragon swallowing its own tail and forming a circle.[198] The Ouroboros often represents self-reflexivity or cyclicality, especially in the sense of something constantly re-creating itself, the eternal return, and other things perceived as cycles that begin anew as soon as they end. From the fourth century BC, Plato tells us in the *Timaeus* that this serpent was self-sufficient, since nothing outside of him existed, so nothing went into or came from him. Movement was right for this spherical structure, and so he was made to move in a circular manner. Because of his own limitations, he revolves in a circle, and from this motion, the universe was created.

From Egypt's Ptolemaic period, the Ouroboro's meaning is also clear, as a symbol depicting self-creation and the source of life: "It slays, weds and impregnates itself." Later, Carl Jung interpreted the Ouroboros as having an archetypical significance to the human psyche. The Jungian psychologist Erich Neumann writes of it as a representation of the pre-ego "dawn state," depicting the undifferentiated infancy experience of both humankind and the individual child. The Ouroboros, the serpent, represents the creative principle of the cosmos, as well as the cosmos itself. It is the Man Cosmos- Schwaller's primordial scission from One to Two, symbolized by the serpent, and their creative relationship functioning in the Number Three. The Ouroboros, however, is not just and ancient mythical symbol. Rather, it is ˙Man's identification with the seamless, eternal state of oneness, whose essence is a deep memory of the origin that words cannot explain.[199]

---

[198] http://en.wikipedia.org/wiki/Ouroboros
[199] Malkowski, E.F. 2007. (p. 384)

The outer circle of the Ouroboros represents the Objective Universe (Circle of Nature). The inner circle represents the Subjective Universe. Between these circles, lies awakened the serpent Leviathan. Some biblical scholars considered Leviathan to represent the pre-existent forces of chaos. In *Psalm 74:13-14* it says, "it was You who drove back the sea with Your might, who smashed the heads of the monsters in the waters; it was You who crushed the heads of Leviathan, who left him as food for the creatures of the wilderness." God drove back the waters of the Earth (*Genesis 1:2*), "And the earth was formless and void, and darkness was over the surface of the deep, and the Spirit of God was moving over the surface of the waters."[200] Leviathan separates the temporal cosmos of the Earth and the spheres of the planets from the Realm of the Fixed Stars and the Realms of Being beyond.[201] The serpent guards the passage between the realms of change and flux, and therefore, the crossing between Objectification (the Will) from the Subjective Universe.

Only two of the Angles (Angles 3 and 4) pierce through the outer Circle of Nature (the outside line of the circle). These are the Gateways between the world of the psyche, the Will and Nature. The outer circle represents the Objective Universe. It is temporal. This cycle has no solution of continuity. It is therefore an "absolute," *nonmanifest* state. Only by virtue of our reason can we suppose the existence of such a state. The circle is therefore ideal, our five senses alone cannot conceive it.[202] It is only when we become conscious of this ideal circuit that a solution of continuity is created.

---

[200] http://en.wikipedia.org/wiki/Leviathan
[201] Rudolph, K. 1998. (p. 69)
[202] Schwaller de Lubicz, R.A. 1986. (p.36)

The Nine Angles

Bear in mind that the Ceremony of the Nine Angles was composed within the "Age of HerWar." It is conceived as a *noetic* vision and expression of Black Magic. The process by which a force not bounded by the rules of space-time-matter-energy comes into being is reflected by the evolution of human thought. The notion of the Third Angle as Understanding implies that a truly conscious being can move beyond Duality (Angle Two). Someone that can only see in black and white cannot synthesize differing ideas. Yet, the "third level" of thinking is, as far as most humans go, hence so many religions are burdened with threes. The Angles work outside these boundaries of normal perception and stretch beyond its limitations.

The magician will soon find that the mythical figures found in the Ceremony of the Nine Angles are based on the writings of H.P. Lovecraft. It is valid to question whether these mythical figures still uphold their value in this day and age. Don Webb explains:

> "Though a half century dead, a number of elements make Lovecraft's work more relevant today than ever: his bravery, his antinomianism, his understanding of how the transformative power of an object (especially a book) can link the realms of imagination and reality, his sense of the cosmic, and finally, above all and unifying all, his insistence on the primacy of the imagination." [203]

It is important for the magician to realize that the Nine Angles are not contemplative ideals, but that they should be put into practice. The actual Ceremony has to be performed in order to

---

[203] http://edred.net/2008/11/why-lovecraft-still-matters-by-don-webb/

manifest its transformative properties. In light of this, we will now introduce each separate Angle, followed by the actual practice of the Ceremony.

- **Angle 1: Chaos**

From the First Angle is the infinite, wherein the laughing one doth cry, and the flutes wail unto the ending of time

Unity - One. The concept of the Universe as the totality of existence.[204] This does not admit to monotheism. The "laughing one" is Azathoth, a mythical figure of H.P. Lovecraft.

The Dream-Quest was the first fiction by Lovecraft to mention Azathoth:

"Outside the ordered universe [is] that amorphous blight of nethermost confusion which blasphemes and bubbles at the center of all infinity—the boundless daemon sultan Azathoth, whose name no lips dare speak aloud, and who gnaws hungrily in inconceivable, unlighted chambers beyond time and space amidst the muffled, maddening beating of vile drums and the thin monotonous whine of accursed flutes." [205]

---

[204] http://www.trapezoid.org/thought/commentary.html
[205] Lovecraft, H.P. (p. 308)

Azathoth is "blind" and an "idiot" because in a condition of perfect unity there is naught else to see, not any knowledge of anything else possible. For humankind, Unity is intelligible, meaning humans can conceptualize and contemplate its existence. Thought always occurs beneath the thinker's essence. So, being below the essence of Unity, man can think of it. Yet, there can be nothing above Unity, so Unity can never think of itself. Therefore, Unity thinks of itself as being nothing else but what it thinks.

In geometry, a singularity identifies a single point only; there is no extension in any direction, for that would produce a line. A point has no dimensions at all.

- **Angle 2: Order**

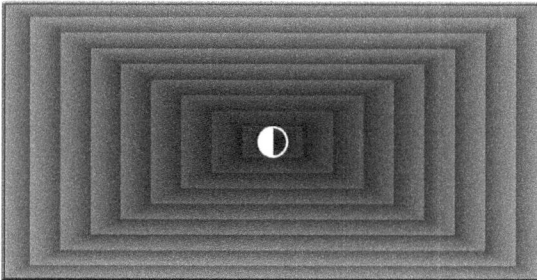

From the Second Angle is the master who doth order the planes and the angles, and who has conceived the World of Horrors in its terror and glory

Duality. The profound and necessarily total change of unity into symmetry and polarity (and its symbolic representations: Horus and Set, *Yang* and *Yin,* etc.).[206] The "orderer of the planes and angles' is Yog- Sothoth, who is, as the shaper of *energy* and matter, described as the author of Earth in its

---

[206] http://www.trapezoid.org/thought/commentary.html

matter/energy/evolutionary configuration. Yog-Sothoth (*The Lurker at the Threshold, The Key and the Gate, The Beyond One, Opener of the Way, The All-in-One and the One-in-All*) is a fictional character in the Cthulhu Mythos and the Dream Cycle of H. P. Lovecraft. Yog-Sothoth's name was first mentioned in his novella *The Case of Charles Dexter Ward* (written 1927, first published 1941). The being is said to take the form of a conglomeration of glowing bubbles.

"Yog-Sothoth knows the gate. Yog-Sothoth is the gate. Yog-Sothoth is the key and guardian of the gate. Past, present, future, all are one in Yog-Sothoth. He knows where the Old Ones broke through of old, and where They shall break through again. He knows where They have trod earth's fields, and where They still tread them, and why no one can behold Them as They tread."

-H. P. Lovecraft, The Dunwich Horror-

In pure duality, there is no room for judgment between the two. The one cannot exist without the other. In duality, geometry creates a line.

- **Angle 3: Understanding/ Conceptualization**

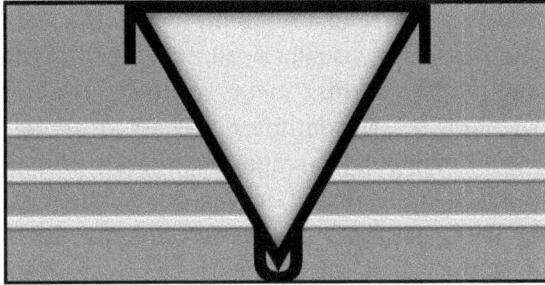

From the Third Angle is the messenger, who hath created thy power to behold the master of the World of Horrors, who giveth to thee substance of being and the knowledge of the Nine Angles

If we look at Three from a mathematical point of view, as an Angle, then One and Two cannot exist without Three. It is the first solid face- a Triangle. Two Angles by itself cannot provide form.

The existence of a third element introduces the notion of choice between the two opposites. This is Nyarlathotep, otherwise Set, otherwise Lucifer/Satan, otherwise Prometheus, otherwise Thoth, who has created the power of perspective and the independent psyche of judgment. Here, knowledge becomes possible.[207]

Nyarlathotep (the Crawling Chaos) is a fictional character in the Cthulhu Mythos. He is the creation of H. P. Lovecraft and first appeared in his prose poem "Nyarlathotep" (1920). The being is one of the cosmic Outer Gods and appears in numerous stories by Lovecraft. Nyarlathotep is also featured in the works of other

---

[207] http://www.trapezoid.org/thought/commentary.html

authors, as well as in role-playing games based on the Cthulhu Mythos.

Nyarlathotep is active and frequently walks the Earth in the guise of a human being, usually a tall, slim, joyous man. He has "a thousand" other forms, most of these reputed to be maddeningly horrific. Nyarlathotep seems to be deliberately deceptive and manipulative, and even uses propaganda to achieve his goals. In this regard, he is probably the most human-like among them. Nyarlathotep enacts the will of the Outer Gods, and is their messenger, heart and soul; he is also a servant of Azathoth, whose wishes he immediately fulfills. Unlike the other Outer Gods, causing madness is more important and enjoyable than death and destruction to Nyarlathotep. It is suggested by some that he will destroy the human race and possibly the earth as well.

- **Angle 4: Being**

From the Fourth Angle is the Ram of the Sun, who brought thy selves to be, who endureth upon the world of Horrors and proclaimeth the time that was, the time that is, and the time that shall be; and whose name is the brilliance of the Nine Angles.

The Ram of the Sun (Shub-Niggurath/Amon) is a manifestation of the "awakened" human psyche as energized by the Messenger. It is thus that "Satan" is known to humanity: a personalized reflection, as it were, of the results of the Messenger's Working.

Shub-Niggurath, often associated with the phrase "The Black Goat of the Woods with a Thousand Young," is a deity in the Cthulhu Mythos of H. P. Lovecraft. The creature is sometimes referred to as "The Black Ram of the Forest with a Thousand Ewe," lending a male gender to the Great Old One that is often thought of as female. The Black Goat is the personification of Pan, since Lovecraft was influenced by Arthur Machen's *The Great God Pan* (1890), a story that inspired Lovecraft's "The Dunwich Horror" (1929). In this incarnation, the Black Goat represents Satan in the form of the satyr, a half-man, and half-goat. In folklore, the satyr symbolized a man with excessive sexual appetites.

Satan's other name (Lucifer) is that of the light bearer, which brings "brilliance" to the Nine Angles.[208] With the number four, we have geometrically a three-dimensional displacement in space. Existence of matter and energy becomes possible. Hence, time becomes possible, as the measurement of change in matter and energy.

---

[208] http://www.trapezoid.org/thought/commentary.html

- **Angle 5: Creation**

From the Fifth Angles are the hornless ones, who raise the
temple of the five trihedrons unto the Daemons of creation,
whose seal is at once four, five and nine

Humanity as the physical vehicle for the expression of the Satanic psyche, provided to us in the Fourth Angle. It represents the concept of the body as a necessary vehicle for the self-realization of the psyche.

Five is quality fully quantified. It is symbolic of the universe manifest, the concept of naturally occurring phenomena being dual in nature and triple in principle. Four accounts only for the concept of matter, five is its creation. In geometry, five creates the pentagram, hence the Golden Section, hence the concept of perfection. This is why to Pythagoras (and his priestly mentors) five was the most sublime of numbers, and why the pentagram was used as the seal of the Pythagorean Brotherhood. Four points of the star represent the animal principle, the fifth represents *manas*, the life force believed to dwell in a person or sacred object. The Ancient Greeks viewed the pentagram as the sacred symbol of light, health and vitality.

- **Angle 6: Death**

From the Sixth Angle is the sleep of the Daemons in symmetry,
which doth vanquish the five but shall not prevail against the
five and the nine

"The sleep of the Daemons in symmetry" refers to the destruction of the Egyptian Initiatory system by Judaism/ Christianity.[209] It vanquished the five (visible tradition), but not the four (the secret traditions of what we have today). This is the accursed (or "hexed") of the Nine Angles. It is the hexagon and hexagram (the seal of the Jews). The hexagon corrupts the Golden Rectangle; it adds an angle and a line to the pentagram and pentagon, thus destroying them. The seeds of the destruction of the hexagonal forms are carried within them. The six-pointed star embraces the spiritual and physical consciousness, viewed by Pythagoreans as the symbol of creation. Interlaced triangles, also known as King Solomon's Seal, portray the union of spirit and matter, male and female. The Seal represents the universe manifest from a central point within the circle of time and space, symbolizing the descent of spirit into matter and its reemergence from the limitation of form.

---

[209] Aquino, M. 2009. (p. 707)

- **Angle 7: Birth**

From the Seventh Angle is ruin of symmetry and the awakening of Daemon, for the four and nine shall prevail against the six

The destruction of the status of monotheism by the addition of a line/angle to the hex. The destruction of Christianity. [210] The legacy of the First Beast of Revelation and his sevenfold Seal and (A.'.A.'.). The forces of the AEon of Horus overcoming those of the AEon of Osiris.

Seven Angles are used as the Seal of Babalon—also known as The Scarlet Woman, The Great Mother, or the Mother of Abominations. She is a goddess found in the mystical system of Thelema, which was established in 1904 with Aleister Crowley's writing of The Book of the Law. In her most abstract form, she represents the female sexual impulse and the liberated woman; although she can also be identified with Mother Earth, in her most fertile sense. Her consort is Chaos, the "Father of Life" and the male form of the Creative Principle. Babalon is often described as being girt with a sword and riding the Beast. She is often referred to as a sacred whore, and her primary symbol is

---

[210] Aquino, M. 2009. (p. 707)

the Chalice or Graal. As Crowley wrote, "She rides astride the Beast; in her left hand she holds the reins, representing the passion which unites them. In her right she holds aloft the cup, the Holy Grail aflame with love and death. In this cup are mingled the elements of the sacrament of the Aeon."

Proponents of six fear that of seven. They warn about such things as the seventh son of a seventh son, of the Seven Towers of Satan in Yezidi legend, of the Seventh Seal, of the Jewel of the Seven Stars. Seven is thus a harbinger of doom to six: a shadowing-forth of the Apocalypse to come.

- **Angle 8: Recreation**

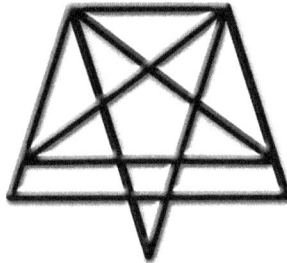

From the Eighth Angle are the Masters of the Realm, who raise the temple of the eight trihedrons unto the Daemons of creation, whose seal is at once four and five and nine

The temple containing the trihedral angles is a truncated pyramid: the power of the trapezoid manifest in a golden Section-based three-dimensional structure. Thus its architects are the Masters of the Realm: the Sorcerers who beam from their towers the Powers of Darkness to rebuild the world corrupted by six and shattered by the seven, and their seal is the Seal of the Order of the Trapezoid (seal of the Priesthood of the original Church of Satan). Angle 8 is linked to Angle 1 (One becomes Two, that becomes Four, that becomes Eight, that becomes One again). Therefore, Eight is a new unity analogues to the first unity, representing renewal or self-replication (recreation).

- **Angle 9: Perfection**

From the Ninth Angle is the flame of the beginning and ending of dimensions, which blazeth in brilliance and darkness unto the glory of desire

The culmination of this dynamic process: the Black Flame in its perfection: the 'Will to power" of Nietzsche in a glory of desire: the extension of the Enlightened Will and Initiated Psyche throughout all dimensions of space, time, and thought: what in the AEon of Set would be uttered as *Xeper.* It represents mental and spiritual achievement. In ancient Greece's Eleusinian mysteries, nine was the number of the spheres through which man's consciousness passed on its way to birth.

Practice

An adapted version of the "Ceremony of the Nine Angles"[211] is provided here. Yet, it is advised that the System be adapted to conform to your own cosmology. It is possible to perform this Working individually, or as a group. It is important to warn the reader here. The Ceremony of the Nine Angles is a noetic method of Black Magic. Once the process is activated, it is impossible to stop. The results are real and will impact your objective and subjective universe, in unexpected ways. Please make sure that you are of sound physical and mental health, before delving into the realm of the Angles.

The Nine Angles should be approached within the confinement of a chamber. The altar should be adorned with the Seal of Runa and a Black Candle. Both music and lighting should be dramatic. Dress appropriately. Participants should distort their human features by using makeup, masks or face-coverings of nylon mesh. [212] Use appropriate incense.

Open the Gates

> Gong x 9, or repeat nine times:
> *"Zazas zazas nassatanada zazas"*

Light the Black Candle

Invocation

> Here it is appropriate to invoke your regular gods/ archetypes (Set/ Lucifer/ Satan, or any other god that features in the Left-Hand Path)

Drink from the Holy Grail

---

[211] LaVey, A.S. 1972. (181)
[212] Aquino, M. 2009. (p. 705)

Summoning of Elements

It is suggested that you summon those elements that make
part of your own tradition

Body

"I am that I am
Through the Angles I speak with the Hornless One
And I pledge anew the Bond with the Daemons
through whose my Will this World is come to Be
As Above, so Below
Let us now also speak the Bond of the Nine Angles

From the First Angle comes Azathoth, the Laughing One
who is Blind and an Idiot
yet, contains the Essence, necessary to manifest Yog-Sothoth

of Angle Two
Yog-Sothoth, shaper of energy and matter
Order our Planes and Angles
Without creating room for judgment
Introduce the notion of choice, without discrimination

Nyarlathotep, Set, Lucifer, Satan, Prometheus, Thoth
Who has created the Power of perspective
as well as the independent psyche of judgment
manifest as Angle Three
and let us drink from its cup without reservation

From the Fourth Angle
The Ram of the Sun – Shub-Niggurath
Manifest the Awakened psyche and bring to us the Messenger
so that I can serve as a physical vehicle of the Satanic psyche

From the Fifth Angle
is brought perfection, sublime in all its forms possible
I stand in the midst of its protection
as the blazing fire of the Pentagram of Set consumes all our
enemies, worthless in their pursuit

and finally destroyed by the Sixth Angle
by addition of a line, so strong in its power
as it corrupts the Golden Rectangle
One plus two plus Three equals Six
reconciliation, peace, presider over crossroads

But lives in fear of the Seventh Angle
that brings it doom to Six
Bring to us completion
We see seven things
We perceive seven movements
We speak seven vowels
We see seven configurations of the moon
Children cut their teeth at seven months
Bring to us the Guardian
The ability to Manifest the Highest in Life
And be fond of it

From the Eighth Angle
manifest the Powers of Darkness
to rebuild the World, corrupted by Six
and shattered by Seven
as it brings into Life the Seal of the Order of the Trapezoid
and brings to us Rhea, the Mother of the Gods
to create for us a Foundation

as the Process culminates from the Ninth Angle
strengthening the Black Flame
the Will to power
Perfection, Xeper
That which brings to completion."

Extinguish the Black Candle

Close the Gate and finish with the words, ***"So Mote it Be!"***

Manifestation of the Nine Angles/ Numbers

The Numbers/ Angles do not manifest in the same linear sequence that they appear in nature (1 to 9). Here we deal with process, each related to a specific Angle and its associated function.

Process One is represented by the Perfection (Angle Nine)-interpenetrating, interacting, interlocked. It emanates from the Absolute, or "central fire," which is the Black Flame. It is the symbolic analog of the original Unity. It is an expression of metaphysical reality. It represents harmony. It is the essence of what brought you here. It is the force that drives our purpose. Yet, it is also the purpose. It is "essence" (therefore, potential) and not "action."

For any action to take place, we need an environment in which to act (a substrate). We rely on our senses to guide us through our actions- our awareness of the physical world, as presented by Process Two- Being. Material, substance, things; the physical world is the matrix of all sensuous experiences. Four represents the basic elements of matter- earth, water, fire and air (wind). It is the *principle of substantiality*.

When we act, we put into motion a process of events, which leads to the concrete Coming into Being/ manifestation of our idea/ project/ thought, etc. This marks the "destination" of our "journey," followed by the process leading to the concrete manifestation of what we would like for to "Come into Being," represented by Process Three- Birth. It is the number of growth. Seven is the seed that through formative growth, becomes the manifest object. It defines the path we take in order to reach our destination (achieve our goals). It is the most difficult of "stages" within the cycle to overcome. It is the point we struggle with, as it presents an obstacle (whether physical or mental in nature). It has to translate to the core of our idea from which manifests the product of our Intent and determines whether we succeed or fail. We experience this as chaos.

174

As humans, we feel restricted by our own abilities. To overcome Seven we need to enter Process Four- Chaos, which builds the foundation for understanding the abstract from which we manifest the concrete. It is linked to the Black Flame (Perfection).

Once we "know what to do" we enter Process Five- the Perfection, the number of "life." It provides the key to the vitality of the universe. Process 5 allows us to create. It is therefore also the number of potentiality, which exists outside time.

From creation comes opposition, presented by Process Six- Order. Two expresses fundamental opposition, polarization. Polarity is fundamental to all phenomena. It brings about order. Without order, there can be no progress. Order does not imply stasis, but rather the knowledge of success. Realization of this creates awareness that we have achieved renewal.

Process Seven– Recreation is a renewal of self-replication. It is an extension of Process 5, as both are creative in nature. It corresponds to the physical world as we experience it.

Yet, we can only enter this Process if we take time to "monitor" the proceeding events, analyze the results and internalize what we have achieved (Process Eight- Death). The actualization of potentiality, within the framework of time and space. It is therefore, called the "Number of the material world." Numbers 1 to 5 are invisible. Six is different. Volume requires six directions. It is a "measure" of the "product." It is the quantification of the results achieved by means of the collective actions of all previous Processes.

We then abstract knowledge and understanding based on Process Nine- Understanding. We cannot know it by the rational faculties, but understand it- love desire, affinity, attraction, repulsion, interaction. The heart, not head, understands Angle Three. Thoth gives access to this knowledge. It brings us closer to a state of perfection, something we will always seek, but never find. You performed an Angle Working,

175

underwent a process with it and gained understanding (consciousness) of it. It is a cycle. It strengthens the Black Flame and leads to further Self-discovery by taking us back to Process One (also Ten), again controlled by the Symbolic nature as represented by Perfection. Seven terms (factors) constitute the cosmos in appearance, whereas nine terms (functions) constitute it as fact. Yet, the psyche is now changed (different). In addition, because the Natural (outer) Cycle is temporal, one can never begin the following cycle at exactly the same point! There is constant change. The time you spent reading this article has caused this cycle to shift.

The Nine Angles, as derivative of the Pythagorean Number System, is more specific, a method of Black Magic. It is a gateway to the Subjective and Objective Universe of the magician. The change it causes is intrusive and not as subtle as those of other Systems. It manifests change in every aspect of our Being, including the physical. Yet, this is not a beginner's guide to practical magic. It is therefore, advised that only those with an advanced understanding of the Self make use of it. The challenges created by using the Angles require a high level of self-control and steadiness. The magician should be prepared to face these changes and bare their consequence. Once activated, it is not possible to reverse or halt these effects, as they are overpowering and the momentum caused by it impossible to resist. This momentum is persistent and provides the necessary energy required by the Magician to free him from the forces of mediocrity. Here, it is not required of the magician to acquire the necessary Will to focus on the manifestation of change, but rather to develop the Will to live with the results.

In the beginning, the Angles manifest anti-poles created by the desires of the Self, in the Objective Realm of the magician. It then pulls the magician into the world he asked for. As a result, the magician is stripped from all familiar support systems and must already be equipped to develop a new survival strategy, based on knowledge of the Self. The method therefore, forces one to develop new skills and competencies. Yet, the Angles aid the magician with this development, by providing a doorway to raw information stored in the individual DNA. It requires much introspection and Self-investigation to find these keys hidden in the DNA, but the results are rewarding. The process fosters a feeling of belonging, as it brings one closer to an understanding of your own genetic makeup, and heritage. Yet, there is a price to pay. Feedback from the DNA also fosters a degree of patriotism. This patriotism is evident in most groups that use the Nine Angles as a Magical System, but be warned that it can be taken overboard.

A number of magicians describe the Angles as a direct gate to the flow of Wyrd (fate- the web of synchronicity and cause and effect), or even flow of time itself. The Nine Angles continuously manifests what Jung coined a synchronicity. It connects the invisible. The Nine Angles accesses both Linear and Angular time and allows the individual to go forth (or back) in time and reconnect at a later stage, bringing back information collected during each journey. It is at this junction that synchronicities manifest in the objective universe of the traveler. The effect is not only immediate, but also very intense. A synchronicity always has significant purpose. It is important that the magician become aware of synchronicities that link to events even before working with the Angles. It is as if the Angles occupy our time long before, and long after activating them.

"Believing, learning and knowing are the three gates of entry into the Temple. "Learning" is establishing, by means of the senses, the reality of what one believes; "believing" is having the conviction about the reality of that which cannot be demonstrated; but truth is the congruity of what one believes or learns- believes and learns- with that, which is. This identification is knowledge, the gate leading beyond the Temple, being within Being.

We may believe in the Universe within Man, we may study the Universe through man, because man is joined with the Universe in man. The identity of the Universe and man is the source of his faith, the source of his science, the promise of his deliverance; it is the knowledge of "the tree at the center."

-R.A. Schwaller De Lubicz-

The Egyptian inscriptions express in various forms the idea that the Temple is the projection of Heaven upon Earth that is upon the world limited by the horizon; the horizon being the line joining Heaven to this world, whether this world be understood as our Earth, or the areas contained within the walls of a Temple, or our own body. In fact, the true living temple of Egyptian Wisdom is Man, who embodies the cosmic principles and function, the Neters. The part played by Theurgy and Numbers is that of selecting and forming individuals capable of aspiring to this ideal type and of conceiving the legacy of the "Ancient Wisdom." Theurgy awakens the latent consciousness by cultivating the power of observation, the recognition of values and the sense of responsibility. This process can better be described by the Egyptian term "Nehast," which literally means to "wake up" to Awaken to the higher existence. It could be summed up in these words: *experience life, look and discriminate.*

Material and Intermediate Sunthēmata teaches us simplicity of heart and Mind (the factor opposed to the complexity of modern thought), and finally the spirit of synthesis, opposed to our analytical mentality. These are the qualities of all true gods. It would not be sufficient to gain access to the "keys" if we did not adapt our way of thinking to their spirit of synthesis and our way of seeing to their simplicity. In this way, everything in us that is corruptible is consumed. Eventually, Noetic Sunthēmata progressively initiates us into the knowledge of the *causal laws*. This leads up to the supreme question of the various destinies of Man as one of the gods. There is certainly only one for us, but the ancients gave him different names according to his forms: when he begets the world, he is *Khepra* in the shape of a scarab; as vivifying king he is Râ, but they put the shape of a viper beside him, whose venom can be fatal; and at the end of the day he is tired, like an old man, and his name becomes Tum. [213] Yet, there is no reason to restrict ourselves to Egyptian lore.

Khepra, the sacred scarab, means *"becoming and transformation."*[214] The scarab is symbolic of self trust and hard work. The beetle goes through very different stages from egg to larva to pupa to beetle. Each stage has its own Work, a particular way of gathering energy and materials, particular ways of transforming them. It senses its own evolution and works toward it—even though the momentum of that evolution will change its shape radically—taking it at the appropriate time into unknown worlds and new modes of Being. [215] The symbol of Khepra remains applicable, even though today we know it as Xeper. Xeper is an Egyptian verb meaning "I Have Come Into Being." Xeper is the experience of an individual psyche becoming aware of its own existence and deciding to expand and evolve that existence through its own actions. These actions lead to experience, from which is derived understanding. Xeper has been experienced by anyone who has decided to seek after his or her own development. Awareness of Xeper usually begins with a moment of rebellion against the spiritual *status quo*. In this sense Xeper is "Satanic." Yet, its properties transcend and are in some ways opposed to that matrix. It is the nature of Self-Creation that it continually re-creates its matrix in the Objective Universe so that the Subjective Universe can evolve and expand.[216]

Theurgy introduces Xeper which, in turn, does not only create awareness of the existence of the individual psyche, but also of the divine qualities thereof. Theurgy literally raises us to the world of the gods, where we can emulate them and finally

---

[213] Schwaller de Lubicz, I. 1978. (p. 61)

[214] Schwaller de Lubicz, I. 1978. (p. 62)

[215] Don Webb. Available from:
http://www.xeper.org/pub/lib/lib_xeper.htm

[216] Don Webb. Available from:
http://www.xeper.org/pub/lib/lib_xeper.htm

become like them, Akhus, walking the earth as giants and accomplishing great deeds such as the creation of the universe! It is only 'as a god' that the Theurgist can partake in the duties of a god. In conclusion:

"Let not such then presume to explore the regions of Platonic philosophy. The land is too pure to admit the sordid and the base. The road which conducts to it is too intricate to be discovered by the unskilful and stupid, and the journey is too long and laborious to be accomplished by the effeminate and the timid, by the slave of passion and the dupe of opinion, by the lover of sense and the despiser of truth. The dangers and difficulties in the undertaking are such as can be sustained by none but the most hardy and accomplished adventurers; and he who begins the journey without the strength of Hercules, or the wisdom and patience of Ulysses, must be destroyed by the wild beasts of the forest, or perish in the storms of the ocean; must suffer transmutation into a beast through the magic power of Circe, or be exiled for life by the detaining charm of Calypso; and in short must descend into Hades, and wander in its darkness, without emerging from thence to the bright regions of the morning, or be ruined by the deadly melody of the Syren's song. To the most skilful traveller, who pursues the right road with an ardour which no toils can abate, with a vigilance which no weariness can surprise into negligence, and with virtue which no temptations can seduce, it exhibits for many years the appearance of the Ithaca of Ulysses, or the flying Italy of AEneas; for we no sooner gain a glimpse of the pleasing land which is to be the end of our journey, than it is suddenly ravished from our view, and we still find ourselves at a distance from the beloved coast, exposed to the fury of a stormy sea of doubts. Abandon then, ye grovelling souls, the fruitless design! Pursue with avidity the beaten road which leads to popular honours and sordid gain, but relinquish all thoughts of a voyage for which you are totally unprepared."

-Thomas Taylor in "Introduction to the Philosophy and Writings of Plato"-

"LITTLE SUNSHINE"

AN AFTERWORD BY DON WEBB

*"I went off to college planning to major in math or philosophy--
of course, both those ideas are really the same idea."*

-Frank Wilczek-

The first time I spoke publicly for the Temple of Set, was at a law enforcement convention. In those long ago days, the fact the Temple of Set had succeeded the Church of Satan made nervous folk picture us as villains from a Hammer film. One of the brainier audience members asked if we indulged in Thaumaturgy. I had no idea what she meant and so said, "Only between consenting adults." I drove home and looked up the word. It was Greek and had been pulled into English by Dr. John Dee. It means *"wonderworking"* or *"doing wizard stuff."* Dr. Dee introduced it in *"Mathematical Preface to Euclid's Elements,"* which appeared in 1570. Dee mentions an "art mathematical" called "thaumaturgy... which giveth certain order to make strange works, of the sense to be perceived and of men greatly to be wondered at."

An art mathematical?

As a writer I thought that magical arts were language driven. I mean, we call them "spells." We have "Words of Power," mantras, chants, and invocations. But with mathematics we have something else entirely. If I write down I saw three bluebonnets blooming today, you know exactly how many (even if you don't have the pleasure of knowing that it is the state flower of Texas). In fact, you can know the number even if you do not know English. In fact, you can know the number even if every single human perishes and you are some visiting alien from Tau Ceti. This would be true as your ability to grasp the Fundamental Theorem of the Calculus or the quadratic formula or (amusingly enough) Göedel's Incompleteness Theorems. Mathematics is where the mind can grasp the stuff of the Cosmos. We need only think of the terrible flash seen on Hiroshima on August 6, 1945, or the beauties of the Mandelbrot set, or watch children play at cutting a Möibus, to understand that math is at the secret heart of the physical world. And that math is the key to *"wonderworking."*

But, math is at the heart of the psyche as well. It is there when a person contemplates the idea that he or she both is and is not one. If I am one, how can I want to do two things – finish this afterword for Dr. Veldman and also go downstairs for my wife's meatloaf? Like all humans, I both crave Unity and enjoy my multiplicity. In most religions man's separateness from the divine is seen as a big problem. The thinkers of Late Antiquity were concerned. "Do I cross into God's realm by his Grace?" or "do I gain my place there by something I do?" The former path to henotheism was popular, the later elite. If I need to cross into the divine realm, I have to make of myself something divine. How do I become One? How do I become the constant in the equation of the universe to which everything else is variable?

If I could make my core like the idea of One, it could be enough. Purely philosophical systems see contemplation as a method of purifying the soul, or even causing an Ascent into powerful regions – such systems generally look upon ritual enactments of Ideas as a "lower" or "superstitious" system. Most magical systems usually think that Ideas are keys to power only through a magical technology. The Setian system (in many ways harkening back to Chaldean Theurgy) sees both approaches as complimentary and necessary.

If you understand the One, you can begin building yourself into a One. If you understand the Two, you have created a soul by forcing the unity of *"Same and Different."* If you can understand the Three, you can begin to control time rather than simply being its plaything. If you can grasp the Four, you have begun to understand what it means to be a center. If you grasp the Five you can understand the body is neither a prison for the psyche, nor more important than the psyche – you can understand that it is a gateway. When you understand the Six, the first perfect number, you can understand how to accomplish all things by doing nothing, or *Wu Wei* – that a perfected psyche changes the Cosmos without "trying." *Wu Wei* means natural action - as planets revolve around the sun, they "do" this revolving, but without "doing" it; or as trees grow, they "do", but without "doing." When you truly comprehend the Seven, you understand that the psyche has internal organization and that you can stimulate certain parts of your psyche and others to overcome even the most terrible odds. When your Mind owns the Eight, you can begin the recreation of the world, relying both on Reason and the Supra-rational. At the Nine, you can achieve Victory -- you are the One reborn into the Eightfold Cosmos of your making.

As humans, with our ten fingers, we love nine. In base ten mathematics, nine is the number that holds itself:

2 X 9 = 18; 1+8 =9

3 X 9 = 27; 2 + 7 = 9 etc.

So, this gives us the great magical toy of 666. In Judaism, 666 is the Cabalistic value of "*Ata yigdal na koach Ado-nai*" or "Now, I pray, let the Power of my Lord be great" (Numbers 14:17). This is Moses' prayer for divine mercy when the Jews were wanting to go back to Egypt and God was pissed off that His Will (Ratzon) was not being done. In Rabbi Eliyahu of Vilna's commentary on the Zohar, there is the idea that 666 contains hidden an exalted and lofty messianic potential. Six is the number of the physical universe - the six directions in Hebrew North, South, East, West, Up and Down. Repeating the number three times reveals that when the Messiah comes he will be able to fully transform the world into a perfect form for those upon it to experience the Creator: 6 + 6 + 6 = 18. 18 is the number, by Hebrew Cabala, for Ratzon (Hebrew Will). This is always linked with Eretz (Hebrew Land) because both derive from the same root(R-tz). In Jewish tradition, it is the Will of the Creator for His people to take over land.

So with Nine, I leave you. You can count Muses, or German Worlds. You can note that this afterword was written in the XLV (45th) year of the Aeon of Set (4 + 5 =9). You can complete the Cycles of the Self, and with the help of this wonderful book, gain some unity. Or, you can merely do some teenage mischief and write "666" on the next piece of currency you hold – and scare some superstitious person with the Number of the Beast, the Number of Man – the Number of a Man whose has decided to Become more than a Man.

6	32	3	34	35	1
7	11	27	28	8	30
19	14	16	15	23	24
18	20	22	21	17	13
25	29	10	9	26	12
36	5	33	4	2	31

The Magic Square of the Sun: 6 X 6 = 36

The first 36 integers: 9 X 4 = 36

Each row is Equal to 111 (the flow of money, sex or magic)

The Sum of all the Numbers is 666, the sign of chosen reality

_____

Don Webb

185

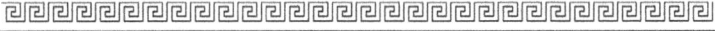

BIBLIOGRAPHY

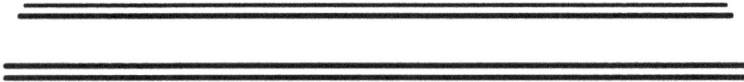

BOOKS AND JOURNAL PAPERS

- Aquino, M. 2009. *The Church of Satan. 6th edition.* 2009. (ebook available from: www.xeper.org/maquino)
- Aristotle, De Caelo, 398 (ebook)
- Blavatsky, H.P. *The Pythagorean Science of Numbers.* Theosophy 1939: 27(7), 301-306, May. (Print)
- *Corpus Hermeticum.* OMTO Series on Esotericism and Spirituality. (Print)
- Crowley, A., Desti, M., Waddell, L. *Magick Book Four- Parts I-IV.* 2nd edition. San Francisco: Weiser Books, 2008. (Print)
- Delatte, A. *Études sur literature pythagoricienne.* Paris: Champion, 1915. (ebook)
- Dillon, J. and Hershbell, J. *Iamblichus- On the Pythagorean Way of Life.* Atlanta: Society of Biblical Literature Text and Translations, 1991. (Print)
- Flowers, S.E. *Hermetic Magic. The Postmodern Magical Papyrus of Abaris.* York Beach: Weiser, 1995. (Print)
- Flowers, S.E. *Lords of the Left-Hand Path.* 2nd edition. Smithville, Texas: Runa-Raven Press, 1997. (Print)
- Fowden, G. *The Egyptian Hermes: A Historical Approach to the Late Pagan Mind.* Princeton, N.J.: Princeton University Press, 1993. (Print)
- Iamblichus. *On the Mysteries of the Egyptians, Chaldeans and Assyrians. Ancient Egyptian Wisdom for our time.* Trans. Thomas Taylor. Miami: Cruzian Mystic Books, 2006. (Print)
- Kingsley, P. *Ancient Philosophy Mystery, and Magic. Empedocles and Pythagorean Tradition.* Oxford: Clarendon Press, 1995. (Print)
- LaVey, A.S. *The Satanic Rituals. Companion to the Satanic Bible.* New York: Avon Books, 1978. (Paperback)
- LaVey, A.S. 1992. *The Devil's Notebook.* Los Angeles: Feral House, 1992. (Paperback)
- Lovecraft, H.P. *The Dream-Quest of Unknown Kadath.* 5th edition (THUS). USA: Del Rey, 1986. (Mass Market Paperback)

- Malkowski, E.F. *The Spiritual Technology of Ancient Egypt. Sacred science and the mystery of consciousness*. Rochester, Vermont: Inner Traditions, 2007. (Print)
- Melchizedek, D. *The Ancient Secret of the Flower of Life*. Vol II. Flagstaff: Light Technology Publishing, 2000. (Print)
- Moore, T. *The Planets Within. The astrological psychology of Marsilio Ficino*. Great Barrington: Lindisfarne Books, 1989. (Print)
- Plato. Timaeus, I, 213:16-18 (ebook)
- Kurt, R. Gnosis: *The Nature and History of Gnosticism*. London: T and T Clark Publishers, 1998. (Google books)
- Schwaller De Lubicz, I. *HER-BAK. The Living Face of Ancient Egypt*. Rochester, Vermont: Inner Traditions, 1978. (Print)
- Schwaller De Lubicz, R.A. *Symbol and the Symbolic. Ancient Egypt, Science, and the Evolution of Consciousness*. Rochester, Vermont: Inner Traditions, 1981. (Print)
- Schwaller de Lubicz, R.A. 1998. *The Temple of Man*. Volumes I and II. Rochester, Vermont: Inner Traditions International, 1998. (Print)
- Schwaller de Lubicz, R.A. *A Study of Numbers. A guide to the constant creation of the universe. 1st US edition*. Rochester, Vermont: Inner Traditions International, 1986. (Print)
- Schwaller de Lubicz, R.A. *Symbol and the Symbolic. Ancient Egypt, Science, and the Evolution of Consciousness*. Rochester, Vermont: Inner Traditions International, 1981. (Print)
- Shaw, G. *Theurgy and the Soul. The Neoplatonism of Iamblichus*. Pensylvania: Pensylvania State University Press, 1951. (Print)
- Uždavinys, A. *Metaphysical symbols and their function in theurgy*. Eye of the Heart: A Journal of Traditional Wisdom. Issue 1, 2008.
- Uždavinys, A. *Voices of Fire: Understanding Theurgy*. Eye of the Heart: A Journal of Traditional Wisdom. Issue 2, 2008.
- Waterfield, R. 1988. *The Theology of Arithmetic* (translated from the original Greek text "*Theological principles of*

arithmetic," by Iamblichus). Michigan: A Kairos Book, Phanes Press, 1988. (Print)
- West, J.A. *The Serpent in the Sky. The High Wisdom of Ancient Egypt.* Wheaton, Illinois: Quest Books, 1993. (Print)
- Williams, C.A. 1999. *Roman Homosexuality: Ideologies of Masculinity in Classical Antiquity.* United States: Oxford University Press, 1999. (Print)

INTERNET RESOURCES

- *Home of Charles Gilchrist.* http://www.charlesgilchrist.com (Accessed 3 July 2009)
- *Ouroboros.* http://en.wikipedia.org/wiki/Ouroboros (Accessed 3 July 2009)
- *Leviathan.* http://en.wikipedia.org/wiki/Leviathan (Accessed 3 July 2009)
- *Temple of Set Homepage.* http://www.xeper.org/pub/lib/lib_xeper.htm
- *Order of the Trapezoid Homepage.* http://www.trapezoid.org/
- *Commentary on the Seal of the Nine Angles.* http://www.trapezoid.org/thought/commentary.html
- *Don Webb Blog at Edred.net.* http://edred.net/2008/11/why-lovecraft-still-matters-by-don-webb/
- *Xeper, the Eternal Word of Set.* http://www.xeper.org/pub/lib/lib_xeper.htm
- *Esoteric and Exoteric, at Kheper.net (by M. Alan Kazlev)* http://www.kheper.net/topics/esotericism/esoteric_and_ex oteric.htm (Accessed 2 January 2010)

INDEX

194

S
SACRED GEOMETRY, 6, 114, 117, 118, 119, 122, 123, 141
SAHU, 91
SAKHU, 91
SANSKRIT, 61, 108, 121, 141
SATAN, 21, 149, 150, 152, 163, 165, 169, 171, 172
Church of, 149, 150, 170
SATURN, 20, 130, 135, 136, 137, 146
SCHWALLER DE LUBICZ, 3, 6, 7, 9, 10, 28, 53, 59, 63, 65, 71, 86, 114, 115, 116, 178
SEAL OF RUNA, 156, 171
SEAL OF BABALON, 168
SEFEKHT, 8
SEKHMET, 97
SESHAT, 56
SET, 30, 34, 48, 149, 151, 152, 153, 161, 163, 170, 171, 172
SETIAN COSMOLOGY, see COSMOLOGY
SEVEN, also see NUMBERS
SEVEN TOWERS OF SATAN, 169
SHABAKA STONE, 31
SHUB-NIGGURATH, 165, 172
SHAKTI, 122
SHU, 8, 30
SIA, 90
SIMPLICIUS, 103
SIX, see NUMBERS

SOL, 128, 129, 130, 131, 132, 134, 139, 145
SOUL, 13, 14, 15, 17, 21, 22-24, 26, 27, 31, 38, 39, 47, 55, 74-83, 85, 86, 90, 92-94, 96, 97, 101-103, 105-112, 115, 125, 126, 127, 128, 129, 130, 131-138, 140, 141, 143, 144, 147-149, 152, 164, 181
Human, 13, 74, 75, 77, 79, 101, 111, 115
Individual, 22, 23, 25, 26
Saturnian, 136
Undescended, 13, 26
Universal, 22
World, 129
SUBJECTIVE UNIVERSE, see UNIVERSE
SUMBOLON, 91
SUN, see Sol
SUNTHĒMA, 80, 107
SUNTHĒMATA, 79, 80, 103, 109, 111, 149
Intermediate, 102, 103, 110, 112, 147, 179
Material, 102, 103, 106, 107, 148
Noetic, 102, 147, 179
SUSTASIS, 94

T
TANTRA, HINDU, 122
TARTARUS, 12, 84, 135
TEFNUT, 8, 30
TELESIOURGIA, 90

www.ingramcontent.com/pod-product-compliance
Lightning Source LLC
Chambersburg PA
CBHW060512090426

42735CB00011B/2189